Negotiate Your Way to Success

Negotiate Your Way to Success

Personal Guidelines to Boost Your Career

Kasia Jagodzinska, PhD

BEP

BUSINESS EXPERT PRESS

Leader in applied, concise business books

Negotiate Your Way to Success:
Personal Guidelines to Boost Your Career

Cover design by Kasia Jagodzinska

Interior design by Exeter Premedia Services Private Ltd., Chennai, India

First published in 2021 by
Business Expert Press, LLC
222 East 46th Street, New York, NY 10017
www.businessexpertpress.com

ISBN-13: 978-1-63742-056-0 (paperback)
ISBN-13: 978-1-63742-057-7 (e-book)

Business Expert Press Business Career Development Collection

Collection ISSN: 2642-2123 (print)
Collection ISSN: 2642-2131 (electronic)

First edition: 2021

10 9 8 7 6 5 4 3 2 1

To the most important people in my life.

Description

The number eight is a special number. It is the symbol of infinity and harmony through the balance of the two interlocking loops. It is considered an allegory of self-confidence, success, inner wisdom, and financial abundance. Number eight means that you are on the right path to reaching your objectives.

I use a guideline as a metaphor for the line by which one is guided to assist the crossover from a difficult challenge to achieving ones' goal. **Negotiate Your Way to Success** is my story line. The line I am passing to you to serve as a foundation for behavior that will deliver what you demand from your professional life and beyond.

Negotiation is both art and a science. A successful negotiation is a balancing act between strategy, tactics, and the right negotiation approach. However, it also relies on the ability to manage oneself. The best negotiation outcomes are the consequences of a coming together of moments and decisions that prove life-changing.

Negotiate Your Way to Success is a collection of pragmatic guidelines flowing from the situations that I experienced working with business professionals across the world. This book is a practical philosophy of personal achievement that I hope will inspire others. While career paths and aspirations may differ, certain professional dilemmas are universal. Bad decisions coupled with good reflections can often produce satisfactory outcomes.

Keywords

negotiation; confidence; career development; success; power; empowerment; self-management

Contents

About the Author

Prof. Dr. Kasia Jagodzinska combines an academic career with international business advisory in the field of negotiations. She served as a Senior Adviser to the United Nations in Geneva, where she provided assistance in multi-stakeholder negotiations and conflict of interest management.

As a professor, she works with students from universities in Switzerland, France, Italy, and Poland. She holds a PhD in International Law, is multilingual and multi-cultural, having lived and worked in several countries.

She is the founder of Negotiation Booster (www.negotiationbooster.com), an innovative approach to business negotiations that leverages the task-related aspects of a negotiation with the underlying emotional factors.

In her role of international negotiation expert, she mentors and trains executives from the biggest corporations in Europe, Asia, the United States, and the Middle East. Working with business professionals from various industries and sectors gave her an in-depth understanding of the professional and personal challenges they face in the interactions with their business partners. Empowering others to succeed and boosting their negotiation power is her passion.

Introduction

I was standing outside one of the most well-known law firms in the business district of the city. Rain was pouring down, and tears were dangerously close to spilling from my eyes. It was at that exact point that I decided to quit my job, with no other secured option. The sky above my head was clouded, but the fact that I did not fit in with the organizational style, the disrespectful boss, the unhealthy atmosphere, and the double morality of the job itself were crystal clear to me. What I did not know was that this decision would be a life-changing one. That spontaneous resignation from the law firm would lead me to develop on a personal level and build a career in international negotiations in the professional field.

My professional track was a series of random events and a winding path of jobs in Paris, Dubai, and finally Geneva. My pursuit of a career in negotiations started that day when I left the law firm and took a job with one of the pharmaceutical companies in Paris. This was a big step for me, both personally and professionally. On the personal level, it meant moving to a foreign country and moving away from my family, which was a difficult thing to do. It was also a career switch from being a jurist to taking over a managerial position in a completely different industry. Given my background in law, my portfolio of responsibilities included, among others, contract review and partaking in negotiations. My responsibilities involved working with partners from Europe, the Middle East, and the United States. What I loved most about the job was the international nature of the business activities and the challenges involved with multi-party negotiations.

Although it took me a total of eight years of studies to get my Doctorate in law, I never really received any formal negotiation training. The business world was my school. It was and continues to be a sink or swim environment. The education process is an ongoing experience. I learn from my clients with whom I negotiate and from the participants of my trainings, just as they acquire knowledge from me.

Apart from the personal challenges that I needed to overcome in order to establish myself as an expert in the field of negotiations, there were multiple obstacles in the professional arena that I needed to face. First of all, I was relatively young when I started my career. I obtained my Doctorate degree at an early age, and whilst I was well-educated, I did not have the practical experience to support the PhD title. During my job interviews, I often heard that I was "over-qualified but lacking practical outlook." Many of the managers I worked with felt threatened by my title, to the extent that I was asked not to use it on my business cards at the beginning of my career. Having to hide something I worked hard for was painful for my young ego. Furthermore, I had to deal with gender-related stereotypes and navigate a volatile business environment in which older men often took the lead role.

My first stop—Paris—was a bumpy ride, but it equipped me with enormous self and professional assurance. In fact, *Paris* is my code word when I think of the moments in my life that brought me immense confidence. What works well for me is the Visualization-Confidence-Realization (VCR) method that I implement in my negotiation sessions. Visualization is the creation of anticipatory emotions. It involves setting a goal, imagining what success will feel like, and directing the efforts toward the desired outcome according to a negotiation plan. Confidence relates to being internally convinced that we deserve what we are asking for and communicating our demands in a clear manner. Realization is putting the plan into action with purpose and conviction.

For example, if you negotiate a salary increase, the visualization part will relate to imagining what you will be able to do with the additional income and how liberating it will be not to have to worry about financial constraints. This is a strong motivator toward the achievement of your predetermined goal (salary increase). Confidence comes from being aware of all the efforts we have put into getting that raise. Many people underestimate their worth or the value of what they do. Realization means asking for what we deserve with conviction. Hesitation in making the demand can lead the other party to doubt whether we merit what we are asking for.

A successful negotiator needs to master the power of subliminal stimuli and focus in order to achieve their desired goals. They need to harness the moment. This book is a collection of guidelines from my career. I am sharing my moments with you in the hope that they will trigger empowering memories from your own experiences. The next time you negotiate, think of a grand instant of confidence in your life. Imagine how invincible you felt then. Now extrapolate that feeling into boosting your inner bargaining power for your future negotiations and life-altering decisions!

GUIDELINE 1

My Career Track Looks
Like an Octopus

I vividly recall one of my first job interviews at a well-known business school. It was the beginning of my academic pursuit, and I was eager to work with the best. Back then, my experience with interviewing for jobs was mainly theoretical. I read many how-to guides on what types of questions one can expect, how to answer them, and what to do to make a good impression. Theory and practice do not always align.

On the day of the interview, I was nervous. On my way to the meeting, I remember thinking that this was my only shot. I could either get the chance of a lifetime or end up playing in the second league, which is how I saw all the other academic institutions back then. In my mind, I was dangerously close to the "Goldman Sachs obsession"—a satirical cartoon about a job candidate fixated on working for this particular bank, blind and deaf to the fact that it might not be the best option for him.[1]

I entered the exquisite premises and took in the sights—the impeccable green lawns, designated parking spaces with personalized name tags for the visitors arriving on that day (my name was there, too!), faculty offices, the academic facilities, the canteen that resembled a five-star restaurant, and of course the centerpiece in the form of the many lecture halls. Everything was designed to maximize the effect of prestige. Even the umbrellas that the people on campus were shielding themselves from the rain with were embroidered with the logo of the school. My subconscious was not oblivious to the status symbols; somewhere in the back of my mind I was registering all these details. This priming was designed to have a universal effect. For the enrolled students it justified the hefty tuition

---

[1] https://youtube.com/watch?v=Lx4poQw1mZo&t=3s (consulted on October 28, 2020).

fees, and for candidates like me it was meant to shape the school into an object of desire. I felt like I belonged there. Impressions are not the best guides since they can be easily manipulated.

As I entered the building, my interviewer was already at the reception desk waiting for me, even though I arrived in advance. We made our way to the meeting room. I felt a wave of emotions sweeping over me. I managed to recall all the things I read about when I was getting ready for this big shot interview. I was careful to choose a "powerful" yet not overly dominant place at the table. I accepted the offer to drink something to show that I am a decisive person who understands their own needs and is not hesitant about expressing them. My hands were on the table, my posture was straight, and I maintained eye contact and a friendly facial expression. I ticked off all the interview-for-dummies tips. Then the interview started. I expected all the regular questions—tell us about yourself, why are you the best candidate for this position, what are your weaknesses (a tricky one), what do you expect your career to look like in x number of years, and so on. I was ready for such questions, including the problem-solving, analytical thinking, or verbal-reasoning skills type. One should also prepare for the unexpected.

The question that hit me like a ton of bricks was when the interviewer asked me to draw my career track. I am blessed to have a few talents. Drawing is not one of them. Nonetheless, without any hesitation, I energetically approached the whiteboard and took a marker. Just as my hand touched the board, the interviewer raised his eyebrows and asked: "Would you like to take a moment to think?" First warning sign that I did not pick up on. In my mind I was already in Picasso mode, no offense to great talents intended. The assignment initially looked like fun, until my mind went blank. I suddenly realized that I am finding it extremely difficult to draw my multidimensional education and professional path. After all, back then, my academic background consisted of a mosaic of legal, literature, and financial management studies. Since it took me a long time to find out what I wanted to do in life, I obtained diplomas in different fields. The more options, the better. Flash forward: The interviewer did not share my opinion.

My professional choices were equally multifaceted; I was bridging managerial activities with academic activities and business consultancy.

How does one draw all that? Most people go for the safe options—the stairs, a logical structure that leads from one position to the next. I was never a fan of linear solutions.

The exercise took some time to accomplish. While I was enwrapped in my artistic efforts, the interviewer was taking notes on my performance. Second warning sign. When I finished, he asked me: "What is this?" I stepped away from the whiteboard to assess the result from a distance. The change of perspective did not make it any easier to answer his question. After some thought, I replied: "It is an octopus." Judging by the result of the interview, this was not the reply he was looking for.

Although it took me some time to come to terms with the decision, this experience taught me a few valuable lessons. First of all, life gives many opportunities, as long as we are receptive to spotting them. Looking back at how my career unfolded, I believe that the universe does have a plan for us. What might initially seem like a failure may be a gentle nudge in another, often better direction. The trick is to keep developing while looking for an environment where you are valued for your unique mix of talents. This proved to be the case for me. My career track is an octopus, and I would not have it any other way.

Guideline 1—Key Takeaways
1. Do not be misled by impression management.
2. Beware of the priming effect and consciously control it.
3. Understand the real drivers of your behavior.
4. Prepare for the unexpected.
5. Think first, then act.
6. Learn how to draw.

Do Not Settle for Less Than What Feels Right

REMEMBER the story about how I quit my job at the law firm? It might seem that the decision was taken on a whim, but in reality, it was the result of several months of internal struggle. On the intuitive level it was a thoroughly analyzed move. Let us go back in time to the origins of why I took on that job in the first place. At any point in time, human behavior is governed by a continuum of needs. A. Maslow referred to this as the Hierarchy of Needs, while negotiation theory depicts five fundamental interests.[2] It might make sense to add the ego to the mix. In most cases, decisions are driven by a multitude of factors, both emotional and rational.

On the rational level, starting a career at a law firm seemed like the logical thing to do, given my legal education. Logic can be limiting. A point worth noting is that creativity should be employed when choosing a career track. Many people will go for the logical option. This means that traditional career paths will be crowded with competitors. Do not be afraid to go out on a limb and explore other options for yourself. Create a niche you can fill with your unique skillset and differentiate yourself from the competition. Even if you decide to choose the logical track, you will feel more empowered by the variety of choices you realize you have off-road. This will greatly increase your bargaining power.

From the emotional perspective, I wanted to continue in the footprints of my Mother. Role models are great, provided you listen to their advice. An objective opinion is often more accurate than what we think is best

---

[2] Fisher, R., and D. Shapiro. 2005. *Beyond Reason. Using Emotions as You Negotiate.* London: Penguin Books. The five interests are: appreciation, affiliation, autonomy, status, role.

for us. Things look different from a neutral stance than they do for the person who is implicated in the situation. It might be interesting to seek a third-party, neutral perspective when you consider your options.

The ego is not the most reliable advisor. It definitely played a part in my acceptance of the job. I was mesmerized by the fancy, modern, slick office, the central location, the reputation of the firm; in other words, by all the artifacts. It certainly was flattering to be offered the job on the next day after the interview instead of having to wait for the decision. That artificial bubble burst fast; they never last long. What is shiny on the outside can sometimes be a façade for rotten internal dynamics and a demotivating work environment, and vice versa. Do not allow artifacts to cloud your judgment.

Mark Twain said, "Find a job you enjoy doing, and you will never have to work a day in your life." That is certainly not how I felt during the months I spent working at the law firm. Each day was a struggle. My life felt like a prison. I had to force myself to enter the office with a smile each morning, while internally I was counting the minutes until the end of each workday. I was surprised when I started getting sick much more often than usual, while I was in good health before. The stress and internal disenchantment were adversely affecting my physical state. Absenteeism, increased employee sick days, and high turnover are usually the first indicators of poor organizational management. The firm certainly ticked all these boxes. I was surprised to find out that the majority of my work colleagues were regulars at the in-house therapist. One might wonder why they needed to have one in the first place …

Things did not feel entirely right from the beginning, and with time that feeling only got stronger. Based on my own experiences and the exchanges with my contacts from all industries and sectors, including academia and business, there is one clear trend that surfaces. If you are not satisfied with your job, you will most likely resign in approximately 14 months. Although research states that most people will have on average two *career* (not job) shifts in their professional path, if you accumulate too many of such 14-month engagements in your CV, you will be labeled a "job hopper." That is not the worse that can happen. The bigger risk that you run when you keep lingering on in an unfavorable situation is that you will develop a perceptual set. According to perception management theory, a perceptual set occurs when you interpret a future similar situation based on your past experiences. If the past is tainted by negative events, you are likely to transplant that negativity to your future interactions. This can be damaging to all your endeavors. Things seldom get better if they do not feel right from the very beginning. Have faith in your instincts. Do not settle until you find the perfect setup for yourself, in both the professional and personal arena.

Guideline 2—Key Takeaways
1. Pay attention to your instincts.
2. Be creative when you explore your career options.
3. Do not be afraid to go off the beaten track.
4. Seek advice from a third party.
5. Control your ego.
6. If you have to settle, settle for more rather than less.

GUIDELINE 3

Set the Bar High

WHILE it is recommended to walk away from less than optimal arrangements, doing so with no other option in sight is an extremely risky move. Actually, risky is a euphemistic term for this type of behavior. Lack of options will leave you exposed, vulnerable, and powerless in the negotiation process. Beggars cannot be choosy. Therefore, if you want to have the freedom and luxury of choosing the best offer, you will first have to create the desire for your offering.

I learned this the hard way. It felt liberating when I quit my job, as if shackles had been removed from my head. That rush quickly faded when reality stepped in, and it was lacking a back-up plan. The market situation was less than ideal; the financial crisis of 2007 to 2008 could not have been a worse time for job hunting. It was an employer-driven market. The volume of job seekers was overwhelming, and employers had free-flowing access to talent at a low cost. People were desperate for employment. Desperation always decreases bargaining power on the part of the one who is asking, both individual and collective.

One could sense the panic. Back then, being interviewed for a job felt like an interrogation. The approach to recruitment and selection was like going fishing with a grenade. It was mechanical and hardly people-oriented. This trend is reflected in the literature. If you look at the titles of books from that time, you will notice a very dry, process-focused approach to the topic. Terms such as human resources or managing capital prevail. Now that the landscape has reversed, companies find themselves having to compete for the best candidates. You will notice book titles changed too—managing talent, investing in people, the power of people, and so on.

A skilled negotiator should pick up on such subtle cues, from both literature and practice. After all, every negotiation is context specific. The negotiation process consists of two parties with common, different, and opposing interests and needs, an object of negotiation (often referred to as a differentiator), and functional proximity. These elements create a system of negotiation, which is embedded in a broader structure (economic or political, or both).

Looking back at when I started interviewing for jobs in this volatile market, I do not think I fully realized what I was up against. In Latin there is a phrase *ignorantia iuris nocet*, which means that not knowing the law hurts. So does not keeping in check with reality in a negotiation process. The feedback I repeatedly received from the recruiters was that I was "over-qualified, not experienced enough, and had too high expectations." Fair point with the inexperienced part. The sacrifice aka concession that I made when I decided to do my PhD in two intensive years was that I did not get a "proper" job during that time. Based on my observation of the colleagues who started the doctoral studies with me and the comparison of dropouts versus those who successfully obtained their degree, I would recommend concentrating on the Doctorate first and then getting a full-time job, provided circumstances allow it. This is critical, especially if time is of the essence, as was the case for me. Otherwise, you will either never get the degree, or it will take much longer to obtain it. The disadvantage is that you will have to make up for the "lost time" and catch up with your peers who already have a head-start in getting business experience. I never regretted my choice, even though the catching-up part took me time and an enormous amount of effort. The trick is to know why you are making a concession and keep your eye on the prize regardless of what the difficulties you encounter may be. One wavering moment of self-doubt can rock the boat and derail you from your objective. To succeed, you will need a lot of personal conviction and support from people whose opinion matters to you.

This takes us to the over-qualified comment. There is no such thing as over-qualified. The more skills you stack, the more plasticity your neurons will acquire. You will be able to more easily adapt yourself to changing market needs by drawing from your potent qualification pool. Naturally, this will differentiate you from the competition and increase your negotiation power in the long run. Remember my octopus career track? One of the fun facts about the octopus is that they have nine brains, one that controls the central nervous system and eight smaller ones in each of the tentacles. How is that for over-qualified?

The juice of the recruiters' feedback and a blessing in disguise was the comment related to high expectations. Statistically, acceptance is just a matter of the number of tries. This means that perseverance supported by (over)-qualifications and hard work will eventually lead you to your desired goals. The path might be winding and foggy at first, which is part of the fun and should be taken as such. Imagine it as a walk through a mist-veiled mountain trail on a beautiful autumn day. There is no greater reward than getting to the peak of the mountain and seeing the sun cutting through the fog and low-hanging clouds.

When you look at the testimony of the most successful people from all spheres of life, one theme prevails: They set the bar high for themselves. Others will respond to the standards and expectations you set and treat you accordingly. They might not always like the value you attribute, but they will respect you provided that you know your value and are ready to stand up for it. If you make concessions for the sake of achieving more, be ready to be rewarded for the things you needed to sacrifice on your way.

Guideline 3—Key Takeaways
1. Create demand for your offering.
2. Pay attention to the context of the negotiation.
3. Know the reason behind the sacrifices you make.
4. "Over"-qualify yourself.
5. Craft many alternative options.
6. Never compromise on your expectations.

GUIDELINE 4

Motivate Yourself to Exceed Expectations

SETTING the bar high means that you will need to be ready to invest a lot of time, effort, energy, and personal sacrifice to reap the desired benefits. Success is not a sprint; it is more like a marathon. To endure, you have to stay motivated. Research shows that motivation is directly linked to job satisfaction. The unfortunate fact is that motivation drops on average by 60 percent after the first year of professional activity. What was initially excitement turns into routine, and soon enough boredom steps in. One might anticipate that a similar problem may exist in other spheres of life. The question, therefore, is how to stay motivated once you set the bar high for yourself.

My students and training participants are a constant source of inspiration for me. They often show me angles of thought that studies alone could never provide. In one of the recent exchanges, I asked my MBA students what their sources of motivation are. I gathered some interesting insights. The answers I collected fell into one of three categories: competition, comparison, and reward. Getting ahead and winning is a strong stimulant, regardless of gender, contrary to what stereotypes may suggest. Competing starts at a very early age, and its first arena is the family circle. No wonder these basic impulses are then transplanted into adult and business life.

Comparing our achievements to those of others is in line with the equity theory of motivation. According to this theory, motivation results from the desire to be treated equitably and fairly. Consequently, people assess their own value by comparing their inputs and outputs to those of others in similar situations: a positive balance results in a higher level of motivation. This suggests that motivation does not exist in a vacuum, but rather is a reflection of how others see us and how we measure against them. The system perpetually fuels itself by the mere fact of operating within societal boundaries.

Motivation can be achieved by both gain and by loss. Taking something away can be a potent stimulant. Behavioral finance suggests that loss aversion is stronger than the desire for acquisition. My experiences indeed confirm the accuracy of this assumption. When I resigned from the law firm, little by little, I was deprived of all the privileges that I enjoyed. I no longer was a member of the *lawyer squad*. I did not have a fancy office with a breathtaking view of the city skyline, my business attire was collecting dust, I stopped receiving invitations to dinner galas and fundraising events, and my networking opportunities were getting dim. My financial resources were melting with each passing day.

That phase of my life when I was interviewing for jobs and facing rejections was by far the worse time in my professional life. I made a vow to myself back then that I would never be in a similar situation again if only I could help it. The loss of my professional identity as I then knew it stripped me off of many things, but it gave me an enormous motivation boost. It made me work that much harder to secure options for myself, sometimes more than may seem reasonable. Loss aversion is what makes me exceed expectations. It is my defense mechanism that stems from the perceptual set I developed while on career rock bottom.

Just like for my students, the reward is a strong motivating factor for me. I always enjoyed discovering the world and expanding my horizons. There are limits even to the things we like doing. The initial rush of starting a new project can quickly fade if the fire is not rekindled. Keeping this in mind, I found two ways to keep it burning bright. When I was studying for my finance degree (which was my least favorite of all my academic undertakings), the exams would be held twice a year and only in designated cities across Europe. My treat was to sign up to an exam center established in a city that I particularly liked or have not been to yet. That would be my reward after a tough examination session and an excuse to discover another culture and customs.

Another motivation trick that works for me is related to Vroom's expectancy model of motivation. According to this theory, motivation is related to the first and second-level outcomes. A first-level outcome is the achievement of a specific goal, for example, closing a good deal with your negotiation partner. Secondary outcomes are those that will be related to that goal—a boost of confidence, recognition, enhanced sense of self-worth, and others. What works for me is to focus on the second-level outcomes—how it will feel to achieve the desired goal.

In today's competitive environment, it is not enough to set the bar high and find ways to stay motivated. Delivering up to the expected standards should be the professional norm. Exceeding expectations is what will make you stand out from the crowd of individuals operating on motivation autopilot. In negotiations, this can be done by leaving a small concession (something of little value for you and of greater value to the other party) for the end of the process. Consider this as a token of appreciation for the mutually invested time and effort toward finding an agreement. Sometimes a small gesture can go a long way.

Guideline 4—Key Takeaways
1. Make motivation a perpetual process.
2. Find out what motivates you most (competition, comparison, reward).
3. Allow loss aversion to fuel you to action.
4. Let second-level outcomes guide you toward your goal.
5. Exceed expectations.

GUIDELINE 5

Success Loves Company

THERE is a saying that goes, "Misery loves company." So does success. Quite often, once you secure one good option, everything else seems to fall into place, and other offers start rolling in. Non-resistance is sometimes the best way of attracting the things that you want in your life. When I quit the law firm job, I started actively interviewing for other jobs. I could not find anything that suited me, or perhaps I was not considered a valid candidate for the positions I was aiming for. Most likely, it was a combination of both these factors. Many companies could not offer immediate employment but promised to keep my application in their records should future opportunities open up. In most cases, this is a swift way of saying we are not interested in your services. Sometimes they actually do what they promise.

Under the harsh market conditions, the search for my new career was taking much longer than I initially expected it would. It was time to pull out the heavy artillery. When I was a student, I worked full-time during each summer break and then part-time when I was writing my two Master theses. I had a solid record and good references from those companies. I decided to reach out to my network of contacts. A pharmaceutical company in Strasbourg, France, that I worked for as an assistant manager was the first one on my list. They were happy to hear from me, but the crisis had impacted them too, and there were no new openings. The regulars were trying to hang on to their jobs. However, its affiliate in Paris, France, did have a vague possibility of employment on a consultancy basis.

It took me a moment to make up my mind. Swift decision making is a desirable skill, one I am still trying to master. Taking on the job meant leaving my family and close ones and starting a completely different life. I was up for changes the day I quit, but this was a different level. I decided to give it one last try in my homeland, although deep down inside,

I knew the decision had already been made. Going into interviews (or any job negotiation) with a lack of conviction and motivation sends a strong signal to the other party. Not surprisingly, my last try proved fruitless. It was time for the big move to Paris.

Establishing myself in the City of Lights was one of my biggest professional and personal challenges. I knew nobody there and decided to move to a residence outside of the city. Choosing quality of life over a minuscule city apartment meant something had to give. That something was easy access to social life. Often times I felt very alone. One of my favorite chill and reflection spots was the outdoor swimming pool surrounded by linden trees. I felt safe there; it reminded me of home and my parents. The move was in May, and nature was in full bloom. The smell of blossoming linden on a late spring evening to this day triggers memories of that special transition time in my life.

It was at the swimming pool, in my serene zone, that I received a call on my mobile phone from an unknown number. Intrigued, I accepted the connection. It was the university in Poland calling. They kept their word and my record on file. Now they were offering me a job. Success indeed loves company. At the time the call came, I was three weeks in the new job in another country. To resign that fast was obviously out of the question. Given my love for academia, it was hard to let such an offer pass. Gain can cause as much of a dilemma as a loss.

I explained to the head of the university on the other end of the line that I had already moved on in my life and had a full-time job. He was not a person who saw things in black and white. "Lecture for us on the weekends in the MBA program," he replied on the spot. That is how I ended up working two jobs (and bridging two different career paths) in two countries on an absolutely crazy schedule. I would finish my work week on Friday night, and while my work colleagues were going out for drinks and dinners in the 8th arrondissement, I was going to the airport. I would take the late-night flight from Paris to Poland, lecture on Saturdays and Sundays, and fly back to Paris on Sunday night. Monday morning would find me back in my office. The notion of a weekend off was nonexistent for me for many months. The travel-light suitcase became my insignia.

The adrenaline of the new experience and gratefulness for job abundance was what kept me going. It was a mind-opening time. I was learning new things in my weekday job by cooperating with business professionals from all over the world. On the weekends, I was exploring the theories that I could then put to the test in my business practice. I was also making a lot of new contacts during the many hours of travel.

This experience taught me the importance of securing one success. Once you manage that (whatever sphere of life it may relate to), this momentum will give you a boost of confidence that will trigger other positive events. The universe resonates with non-resistance; it responds to your relaxed and serene energy. So do your negotiation partners or the people you wish to influence. The first success starts the domino effect. When you modify one behavior, it will activate a chain reaction and cause further behavioral changes. It is a bit like the expectancy theory we discovered in Guideline 4. The successful first-level outcome resulting from a given effort will pull along second-level effects. Knock over the first pawn, no matter how small it may be. The next ones will fall automatically.

Guideline 5—Key Takeaways
1. Secure one success and the next one will follow.
2. Attract what you want by letting go.
3. Do not be afraid of change; this is when it all starts.
4. Be open to creative arrangements; they will open new doors for you.
5. Accept that (temporarily) life-work balance may be a myth.

GUIDELINE 6

Get the Best Job Title

HAVE you ever noticed how proudly people present themselves in business interactions? I am not referring to those situations when you meet someone new, and they introduce themselves with their birth name. What is more intriguing are those cryptic titles that you can never remember nor fully comprehend what they stand for. Here are a few examples that I encountered in my practice: field enabler manager (responsible for providing tools, training, and content for field managers), talent delivery specialist (recruitment manager), under-secretary to the sub-committee (no idea what tasks and responsibilities that designates), scrum master (idem), or alternatively Chief Human Resource Officer (CHRO) of ... a one-person company.

Jokes aside, a title becomes your professional identity card. It reflects your status, as well as the investment and sacrifices you made to get to a certain level. No wonder people develop an ownership effect concerning their job label. One of the best pieces of advice that my mentor gave me when I was interviewing for the job in Paris was to negotiate the best title. Back then, I did not fully understand the future implications of what seemed to me a futile linguistic exercise. There were more critical aspects, such as remuneration and career growth possibilities. Nonetheless, I had faith in his professional judgment. Today I cannot thank him enough for looking out for me in that small but powerful detail. To this day, I remember to follow his counsel in each new appointment and job I accept.

A job negotiation consists of a jigsaw of elements, such as the salary level, additional benefits, training and development options, flexible work time, career advancement opportunities, health insurance, access to company assets, travel in style packages, and many others. A savvy negotiator will place the job title at the top of the list of their demands. A negotiation is an exercise in trade; you give away something of less value to you in exchange for something that has greater value. The more demands you prepare and bring to the table, the more opportunities for the trade you have. If you need to make concessions, make sure that the job title is not one of them.

The title you kickstart your career with or the one(s) you held in your previous job(s) will be your springboard to your next position(s). Many search engines are designed to pick up on keywords: manager, professor, consultant, and so on. If your curriculum vitae or profile on professional networking sites lacks certain buzz words, exciting business opportunities may pass you by. Enigmatic functions may put off potential business contacts. Mitigate that effect by making your title clear, universal, and easily understood. Try obtaining the highest possible rank, even if it means making a temporary concession on the salary level. In the long term, you will find that you can more easily increase your remuneration than enhance your professional title.

Furthermore, titles are a reflection of expertise power. They designate you as an expert in a given field, and increase your external credibility. This can have a substantial effect on the way others perceive you. Notice what happens when the so-called *experts* are invited to a negotiation or any other type of discussion. People naturally react to authority. Consequently, they are more prone to behave according to the expert's opinion. They assume that the person possesses higher-level skills and knowledge. The title becomes a professional shield.

Lastly, labels are a self-fulfilling prophecy. Their power is inward-oriented. The acquisition of a specific title will lead to a modification of your behavior. Just as others' perception of you will change, so will your own. You will carry yourself differently. A sophisticated title will make you want to live up to all the connotations related to the rank you hold. A title that you worked hard to get is an obligation to fulfill certain expectations linked to a specific role. Remember that the title affects the mind, but do not let it go to your head.

Guideline 6—Key Takeaways
1. Avoid cryptic titles.
2. Never accept a lower title in exchange for a higher salary.
3. Choose a clear, universal, and easily understood title.
4. Negotiate the best possible title.
5. Let the title be a source of your inner power.

GUIDELINE 7

Never Stop Looking for New Career Opportunities

IT takes approximately two months for a new behavior to become automatic and anywhere between 18 to 254 days to form a habit. The latter period depends on several factors, such as personal characteristics, intensity and type of the action, substances (or lack thereof) involved, and others. No wonder that my daily routine of looking for a new job after I left the law firm became second nature to me. During that time, I implemented a similar schedule to fill up my days. It prevented me from procrastination and introduced a structure to my new reality. Each morning I would refresh my mailbox hoping for a message of acceptance, then I would check on the status of the applications I submitted, and finally I would proceed with screening job ads. The rest of my day would be spent networking with business contacts or prospects, attending career events, or going for job interviews.

When I moved to Paris and settled in the new role, I was surprised to find that surveying the job market continued to be an item on my agenda. My morning hot chocolate and croissant were accompanied by the latest newsflash and a quick review of the job market. It was as if I needed to keep my options open. Knowing that there are multiple possibilities on the job horizon brought me a sense of comfort. Clearly, job searching had become my habit. Hardly the worst one.

To successfully navigate the job market, negotiation skills and tactics are often not enough. I learned it the hard way that if you enter a job negotiation with fear, self-doubt, or lack of conviction, you will not win no matter how well tactically you have been prepared. The interviewer will automatically pick up on the low vibes you send out. To land (or create) a job of your dreams, you will need to leverage the task-related aspect of the negotiation with the underlying emotional factors. Success starts with self-management.

To radiate an aura of confidence, you will need to develop strategies for personal empowerment. Knowledge is power. Build up your courage by equipping yourself with insights about the overall condition of the market and state of the economy, specific job requirements for candidates, the constraints that companies are facing (such as shortages of the workforce, for example), as well as any other factors that can affect the job market. A job advertisement is a goldmine of this information. All you need to do is read between the lines of what companies are looking for to start to notice certain trends and patterns.

Once you have done your research, proceed with an analysis of your portfolio of competencies and an inventory of your personal skills to see how you can supply the demand. Do not downgrade any of your talents or life experiences, even if they are not strictly professional. At a minimum, each person operates in a given societal frame. This means that we all deal with other people. Consequently, this translates into communication skills, conflict management capacity, ego and stress management, and human relations management, to name just a few *managerial* skills.

Once you know what the market needs are and what you can offer, you will notice that there are multiple options to choose from. You can apply for a job or fill a niche with your unique skill set by setting up your own business. Be creative. Somewhere there is a need for your product or services; you just need to find it. The more options you realize you have, the greater your bargaining power will become. A job candidate who is well aware of the existence of valid alternatives enters the job interview from a position of strength. Woody Allen once said that 80 percent of success in life is showing up. Show up as the winner that you are, and you will be treated as such.

Through the years, I have cultivated my habit of screening for jobs. I find that it has saved me from feeling like a hostage of a given career in many situations. Whenever I feel trapped, I always remind myself that there are other options. Having a choice is the ultimate form of freedom and independence. You do not need to execute the choice; it is sufficient to know that it exists. The trick is to look for new career opportunities perpetually. To craft them under the pressure of the moment is a moment too late.

Guideline 7—Key Takeaways
1. Make career searching a life-long habit.
2. Develop strategies for personal empowerment.
3. Equip yourself with information about the job market.
4. Make an inventory of your knowledge, skills, and abilities.
5. Craft multiple creative options for your career.

GUIDELINE 8

Develop Your Natural Talents

THE second runner-up on my list of "favorite" interview questions that I compiled during my interviewing crusade was to talk about my main weakness (the first one was, of course, the career drawing). Since an interview is not a court hearing, I never felt compelled to tell the truth and nothing but the truth. Neither should you be. The cliché way out of this tricky situation is to talk about a vice that is disguised as a virtue and does not affect the job you are applying for. Banalities seldom serve any higher purpose, neither for the interviewer nor the interviewee.

Some say that focusing on weaknesses can help you grow and develop. I disagree. It is much more productive (and enjoyable) to enhance your natural talents. We all have a finite amount of energy and self-discipline. If we channel all our attention to correcting weaknesses, sooner or later, something will have to give. It is only a matter of time before demotivation steps in. Therefore, limited resources need to be distributed wisely. Efficiency theory states that peak performance is achieved by using the least amount of inputs to achieve the highest amount of output. Consequently, focusing on utilizing your talents will increase the chances of obtaining your desired objective in the long run.

I always liked the saying, "Love what you do and do what you love" (Ray Bradbury). It is such a positive and liberating message that it can serve as a guide for your career choices. Since you will spend the majority of your time working, would it not be better to occupy yourself with something that you actually enjoy doing? This revelation was the proverbial drop that spilled the glass for me when I decided to quit my law firm job. At one point, I found myself wondering, "Is this all there is to work life?" The vision that this state would continue for the foreseeable future frightened me, but it also and gave me a boost to alter my career track. Once that question pops up, there is no turning back. Change is only a matter of time.

Ironically, finding out what you truly like (and making a living out of it) is not as easy as it may seem. My law firm experience taught me that you first know what you do not like. If you are hesitant and consistently weigh the pros and cons of a given situation (with the scale tipping to the latter), this most likely means that you have not yet found your true calling. Once you do, you will have no doubts. It will simply feel right.

It might be helpful to first understand what talent, to then develop it. Most resources define it as a natural aptitude, ease of doing things that comes effortlessly. By contrast, a skill is an acquired ability, something that requires an investment of effort. The Oxford Languages Dictionary provides a second definition according to which talent is a former weight and unit of currency, used mainly by the ancient Romans and Greeks. Make your natural talent your career currency.

Guideline 8—Key Takeaways
1. Focus on your strengths, not weaknesses.
2. Distribute your energy in the most efficient manner.
3. Find out what you do not like and make a change.
4. Discover what you enjoy doing (and what you are good at).
5. Maximize your natural talents.

Build Your Army of Supporters

WHEN I moved to Paris, I did not know anyone except for the HR director with whom I had the job interview a few weeks back. The first piece of advice I remember receiving over a welcome lunch with my work colleagues was that I need to find a savvy lawyer, a creative tax advisor, and a good dentist. Fair enough. If only that were enough to set one up in life …

It takes hard work to build a network from scratch, but it would be even more difficult having to go through life without a secure base of supporters (that includes more people than a lawyer, a tax advisor, and a dentist). It takes time and patience for people to open up and trust since trust is built by spending time together and jointly overcoming the obstacles in life. This is how you prove yourself to the other person and show your true colors.

In the iconic movie *The Godfather*, Michael Corleone utters the famous words to Sonny: "It's nothing personal, it's strictly business." Business has become personal; perhaps it always has been, and Al Pacino's character was mistaken. People want to do business with partners on whom they can rely. If trust is established, it becomes much easier to agree on the merits of a given case because the energy can be directed towards the common goal instead of testing the other person. Therefore, long-term and sustainable agreements require a well-balanced ratio of task execution and relationship building.

The question then is how to assemble your forces. Indra Nooyi, the former CEO of Pepsico, was asked in one of the interviews what her recipe for success is. Her reply was not what one would expect from someone who ranks among the 100 most powerful women in the world. The advice she gave was people-oriented rather than strategic: "Assume positive intent." What a heart-warming reply and one to live by. The world is a mirror. If you react to others from a positive perspective, they will be attracted like magnets by your positive energy and good vibes.

The law of reciprocity is a vital factor in building a network of supporters. Remember to treat people the way you would like to be treated. Courtesy and respect are fundamental human rights. Applying them serves as testimony to your own standards of excellence and places you in the position of a leader who sets the criteria for the relationship. Find something you genuinely admire about the other person, no matter how small it may be. Everyone likes to be appreciated. Appreciated people become supporters.

It is generally recommended to give more than you take. Psychology studies confirm that the act of giving stimulates the hormonal production of the happiness trifecta—the trio of dopamine, serotonin, and oxytocin. Giving has a positive effect on both the body and mind. The side effect may be a larger base of supporters. On the contrary, taking may elevate stress levels because it creates a feeling of being indebted. If you need to ask for something, ask for advice to boost the sense of the importance of the other person.

Throughout my business and academic practice, I noticed that young professionals are often hesitant about using their networks for support. They feel that relying on their contacts would give them an unfair advantage in the market. I respect a strong work ethic more than anything else. However, a stable network of contacts proves that you are a reliable partner with whom people want to be associated. Otherwise, they would not risk their own reputation to vouch for you. A substantial army of supporters is your reward for the investment you made when building and nurturing it. Do not refrain from claiming your prize.

Guideline 9—Key Takeaways
1. Invest time and have the patience to build trust.
2. Remember that business is personal.
3. "Assume positive intent."
4. Apply the law of reciprocity.
5. Give more than you take.
6. Rely on your network for support.

GUIDELINE 10

Get a Tough Mentor

WHEN I joined the company in Paris, my academic track was greatly outweighing my business experience. About a month in the new job, I had a chat with a senior executive who flew in from one of his frequent business trips. The topic of our conversation turned to career development. He seemed trustworthy and empathetic, so I opened up about my recent job-hunting experiences. I told him how demotivating it was to have multiple academic degrees topped with post-graduate certifications, a command of several foreign languages, and still have to struggle to get a good job. At first, his reply made me question my judgment of human character. "Congratulations, you can work the counter at one of the boutiques on Champs-Elysees," he riposted. This was certainly not what I was expecting to hear. That was the moment I found my business mentor.

If you watched any of the classic action thrillers, specifically of the genre that involves a hostage-taking situation, you might have noticed that the negotiator is often reinforced by a commander. The role of the latter is to offer support to the negotiator. Because the commander does not directly partake in the negotiation, they have an objective, neutral overview of the situation. This allows them to serve as the emotional balcony—a secure place where the negotiator can go to regain balance in case things get heated. This is logical because it is not possible to be both emotional and rational at the same time. The moment you get involved in the action is the moment you lose your objective stance. The model of team division of commander and negotiator has been introduced by the FBI and adapted to modern business practice. In circumstances other than difficult negotiations, the commanders are usually called mentors. They need to be tough.

My *extra-professional* mentor is my Mom. She is my biggest supporter, someone whom I look up to, and the only person to whose command I completely surrender. Her parental strategy is tough love. Somehow, she mastered the art of always being there for me, but at the same time not smothering me with affection. I remember the one and only time she allowed complete vulnerability was when I lost a dear friend. In all the other moments of hardship, she would pretend like nothing wrong was happening. Only a very skilled observer would notice all the emotions that were crashing through her like waves. Her calm demeanor and no-nonsense attitude set me straight each time and gave me the strength to overcome even the most challenging situations in life.

Writing this part, I am reminded about the uplifting poem "Footprints," also known as "Footprints in the Sand." It beautifully grasps the essence of what a commander is:

One night a man had a dream. He dreamed he was walking along the beach with the Lord. Across the sky flashed scenes from his life. For each scene, he noticed two sets of footprints in the sand; one belonging to him, and the other belonging to the Lord.

When the last scene of his life flashed before him, he looked back at the footprints in the sand. He noticed that many times along the path of his life there was only one set of footprints. He also noticed that it happened at the very lowest and saddest times of his life.

This really bothered him and he questioned the Lord about it.

"Lord, you said that once I decided to follow you, you'd walk with me all the way. But I have noticed that during the most troublesome times in my life there is only one set of footprints. I don't understand why when I needed you most you would leave me." The Lord replied, "My precious child, I love you and would never leave you. During times of trial and suffering, when you see only one set of footprints in the sand it was then that I carried you."[3]

Do not be tempted to take the easy road. Proper mentoring that will help you thrive is not a walk in the park. Choose a mentor who is compassionate but not overly emotional. Compassion does not mean that you both dwell in sorrows. By not allowing you to succumb to your woes, a commander will teach you self-management and emotional discipline. The best thing that they can do for you is to keep their composure; this way, you can draw from their vivacious energy and stabilize yourself. Two negatives only make a plus in mathematics.

---

[3] Author Unknown.

A good mentor will be an accurate judge of your character. They need to understand your skillset and push you to develop your natural talents. Last but not least, they should know what makes you click. For example, my business mentor (and dear friend) is well aware that I like things to be well organized. As the COVID-19 showed, there is only so much one can plan in life. Each time I was working on a project (such as writing this book during the pandemic, for example), he would urge me on by reminding me that in this challenging time, the chapters were the only thing under my complete control.

Guideline 10—Key Takeaways
1. A mentor is like a commander—they are your security blanket.
2. They need to be emotionally stable to be able to stabilize you.
3. Choose someone you will trust and see as an authority figure.
4. Rely on their judgment—things look different from an objective view.
5. Tough love will make you stronger.

GUIDELINE 11

Never Compromise on Your Values

CONTRARY to what inexperienced professionals might think, compromise in negotiations is not a win-win solution. In fact, it is a win-lose strategy, which means that you lose something, and you gain something, usually half of the available resource. Some say that obtaining half is better than having nothing. That logic fails to consider the other aspect of the equation—what you might have to give up for the gain. Some things cannot be quantified by monetary value, or the price may simply be too high.

One of the most significant risks of this approach is that once you compromise, you start crafting a pattern of behavior for yourself, and you send a particular signal to your negotiation partner. Remember that you are the one who sets the expectations, and only you can decide to lower them. The moment you compromise is the moment you open the door for further exploiting, both internally and externally.

At the beginning of the book, I mentioned some of the reasons behind my decision to quit the law firm. The despotic organizational style, the disrespectful boss who created an unhealthy atmosphere, and the double morality of the job itself were all factors that went against my personal values. It felt uncomfortable to work in an environment that lacked alignment with my inner system of beliefs.

I often witnessed injustice toward my colleagues or was placed in situations that would require me to resort to double morality standards. One of the (many) turning points for me was when I witnessed the boss physically abusing his dog during one of the weekend team-building events. A person who takes out their anger issues on a powerless creature will have no scruples when it comes to mistreating people. The poor animal was terrified, similar to half of the team who saw the act of cruelty. There are some things you simply should not turn a blind eye to.

In conflict management theory, values are one of the key elements of the wheel of conflict. According to Mayer:

Values are the beliefs we have about what is important, what distinguishes right from wrong and good from evil, and what principles should govern how we lead our lives. (...) Because people define themselves in part by their core beliefs, when they believe these values are under attack, they feel they are being attacked. Similarly, it is hard for people to compromise when core beliefs are in play, because they feel they are compromising themselves or their integrity. [4]

Management literature places a strong focus on the notion of a work-life balance. This concept is criticized by some experts, and even more so by practitioners, many of whom have realized that it is an idyllic approach, aka an urban business tale; someone somewhere has managed to achieve it. There are specific periods in your career when something will have to give, either life or work. In order for that something not to be your values, you need to instead find a *work-life fit*. Find or craft a job that will not require you to modify your values or stretch your beliefs beyond the limits of your ethical framework. No job is worth the sacrifice of your dignity, no matter its temporary rewards.

Your values are your internal ID system. They are what makes you unique and distinguishes you from the competition. Just like goodwill is one of the most valuable non-monetary assets of a company, your values constitute the fundament of your personal brand. Long-term relations are established only with partners with whom we are aligned on the moral level and whom we can rely on. Cut off situations that risk chipping away at your integrity immediately, or better yet, do not even get involved in any, if possible. Compromising on your values is like a crack in glass; once broken, it will shatter to pieces with time.

---

[4] Mayer, B. 2000. *The Dynamics of Conflict Resolution*. A Practitioner's Guide: Jossey-Bass.

Guideline 11—Key Takeaways
1. Compromise is a win-lose strategy.
2. No gain is worth the loss of your personal values.
3. Build and protect your integrity.
4. Find a work-life fit.
5. Cut off situations that are detrimental to your system of values.

Design Your Personal Brand of Excellence

THE less known Greek islands host some of the most breath-taking getaway spots. The natural landmarks combined with a mythical atmosphere attract people from all over the world. Some go there to soak up the sun; others end up embarking on a spiritual or intellectual journey. It was on a Greek mid-summer evening somewhere in the middle of the Aegean Sea that I learned a valuable lesson on personal branding. Business never sleeps, it seems.

On one evening during a vacation with my colleagues, we went out for what turned out to be a memorable dinner. Having spent an active day, we decided to opt for the in-house entertainment offering. The hotel we were staying at had organized a small concert for their guests that evening. We found ourselves dining by the beach to the accompaniment of live music. The band consisted of a group of musicians from Australia. The young men were island hopping in the hope of making a name for themselves in the musical arena. They were playing remakes of old and new classics mixed with their own music collection.

As expected, the food was amazing, but it was the musical setting that made for an interesting experience. The lead singer had the type of voice that can bring shivers to one's spine. He perfectly conveyed the emotions encoded in the popular hits he chose to sing. Soon enough, he had the whole crowd humming along and swaying to the rhythm. My friends and I were enchanted by the beauty of his vocals and the clever selection of all-time favorites. He then weaved in his own repertoire of songs. It took only a few musical pieces to break the spell we were under.

Suddenly the whole vibe changed; the lead singer's voice was still beautiful, but it now lacked confidence and passion. The audience soon became distracted and then non-receptive. People turned to their drinks and dinner conversation. Judging by the weak power pose of the artist, he sensed that he had lost his grip over them. The show ended with a moderate round of applause. People have a short-term memory.

It took us a moment to realize that we had just witnessed a *personal branding meltdown*. When the concert was over, my colleague walked up to the young man and said to him: "Your performance of the classics was amazing. You are extremely talented. Why do you not sing your own songs with the same conviction that you have when you sing the songs of others?" Great point and an equally applicable one outside of the music industry.

The most frequent concern expressed by the business professionals in my negotiation trainings is that they are not in a position of power. They see themselves as inferior to the boss who calls the shots. Somehow, they have managed to convince themselves that they are in a relationship of dependency with no options or way out. It never ceases to amaze me how high-profile experts can downplay their own status and ultimately end up taking away their own power. In that regard, they are no different than the artist who rocked all the songs except his own.

Negotiating is like being on stage. You have to have a command presence to captivate your audience. If you enter a negotiation with anxiety, self-doubt, or lack of belief in success, you will not win even if you have strategic preparation. My book entitled *Negotiation Booster: The Ultimate Self-Empowerment Guide to High-Impact Negotiations* provides more insights on this topic. It equips the readers with a selection of strategies for thriving in negotiations by means of directional self-management and personal empowerment.

We all have unique talents, skills, and competencies that we put to use in the service of others with ease and dedication. The majority invests their time and efforts in helping to develop entities that are not their own making. They spend their careers singing remakes of old classics. Why not channel that energy into the design of your personal brand? This does not mean that we all have to be entrepreneurs; there is nothing wrong with the preference for the stability of being on the payroll. However, only by recognizing and claiming the value you bring to your company, organization, or unit can you become indispensable. If you manage to build your own brand of excellence, you will never again doubt the power that you hold, whether in someone else's organization or beyond.

Imagine that you are working in the service of your personal brand. Make it your job to be a worthy representative of yourself, just as you would support and promote the company you are working for. Do not be like the musician who makes an unforgettable performance only when he sings remakes. Shine with equal passion and conviction when you present your own repertoire.

Guideline 12—Key Takeaways
1. Use your unique skill set to build your own personal brand.
2. Do not allow yourself (or others) to downplay your status or downgrade your power.
3. Enter a negotiation with command presence.
4. Work in the service of your personal brand.
5. Let your personal brand play first chair.

GUIDELINE 13

Expand Your Horizons

MANY young professionals share a similar concern—it takes them some time to figure out what they want to do in life after they graduate. This is not uncommon and can happen at later stages in the career as well. Knowing what you do not like precedes knowing what you like. Not knowing neither is where it gets a bit tricky. During my university years I found myself in the latter category. I was doing two Master degrees simultaneously, and although this was a strenuous exercise, I was not looking forward to leaving the academic bubble. What better way to prolong the student-life bliss than by continuing the studies? Therefore, I decided to pursue my Doctorate degree in law. Postponed decisions will eventually catch up with you.

As with any endeavor, there were supporters and fierce critics of my decision. The latter category prevailed. Their main argument was that the time I would invest in my studies will be sunk time in terms of gaining professional experience. Fair point, but only to a certain extent. A way of mitigating that risk is to channel all your efforts toward your designated goal. This was precisely what I did. My strategy was to get a scholarship for my academic achievements to financially support myself. This would allow me to concentrate solely on obtaining the degree in the shortest time possible, with no other distractions.

The majority of the other PhD students with whom I enrolled in the program juggled between their jobs and studies. The result was that I obtained my degree in two years, while some of my colleagues either dropped out or took double that time to finalize the procedure, in the best cases. Success is the result of external and internal factors coming together. It takes unwavering motivation and perseverance to multi-task. One also needs a favorable environment that will support goal attainment, which usually means access to financial time and energy resources. That is why sometimes it is better to make hay while the sun shines.

Freedom comes at a price, usually calculated in doubling the standard effort you would typically need to invest. When I entered the job market, I was two years behind my peers in terms of professional experience. This meant light-years in a volatile and highly competitive business arena. The law degree was initially a roadblock for me because I chose a career track outside of the standard academic parcourse. My toll was an intensified effort to catch up, which meant getting a job and simultaneously (this time) starting a professional degree in finance. Catching up is not enough; you need to exceed expectations.

Indecision can have upsides, provided you channel it well. My hesitation in career choice allowed me to expand my horizons beyond what I most likely would have if I had opted for the classic staircase work model after my Master studies. Instead, I could happily draw an octopus in one of the more memorable job interviews.

Apart from gaining more neuroplasticity, expanding your horizons will help you build up a talent stack and establish a unique position in the job market. In an ever-changing business environment, the more skill sources you can draw from, the more equipped you will be to adapt to the changing conditions and requirements. Narrow specialization is a luxury of only a few professions.

In negotiations, one of the biggest sources of bargaining power is the existence of alternatives. The more skills and talents you possess, the less dependent you are on one job, employer, or even career path. There is no greater freedom than the freedom of having a choice. Build your personal brand by getting a broad range of expertise, and people will flock to you for the knowledge you hold and the power that comes with it.

Guideline 13—Key Takeaways
1. Keep developing even if you are not yet clear about what you want to do.
2. Once you set a goal, channel all your efforts to achieve it.
3. Invest time in the most efficient manner.
4. Be ready to pay the price for going off the beaten track.
5. Build up your unique talent stack.

Learn to Live One Day at a Time

THE initial title planned for this chapter was "You do not need to know where you will be in five years." It was triggered by the memories of the numerous job interviews during which I was asked a variation of the cliché question about where I see myself in the next x number of years. There are at least two things that are wrong with this query. Firstly, it forces the interviewee to engage in creative storytelling (aka lying). The apparent answer "in your job" is most likely not the one they are looking for. Secondly, it invites the candidate to immerse in an illusionary belief that we are the masters of our future. "If you want to make God laugh, tell him about your plans" (Woody Allen). An interviewer who poses such questions may be perceived as either unethical or delusional, or perhaps they simply enjoy a good joke. Not necessarily do they merit to be your employer of choice.

The COVID-19 crisis led to a worldwide meltdown of the health, social connectedness, and the economic system. The uncertainty and loss of sense of control caused havoc on the individual level. It stripped people of the illusion of being the shapers of their own destiny. Due to recurring lockdowns, regulations changing overnight, and the introduction of new (and often confusing) restrictions, it became impossible to plan what one would be doing the next day or week, not to mention in several months. From a collective mindset oriented on long-term planning, people had to abruptly learn how to live one day at a time. The established social norm of well-organized and durable time horizons collapsed. Ironically, being well-organized and dependent on a fixed schedule proved to be a hindering factor.

The pandemic shed light on an interesting phenomenon—the inability to live in and for the moment. Had this ability existed, people would not have gotten so agitated about the sudden loss of command over the long-term angle. After all, the moments that life consists of did not change; only the longevity aspect of their sum did. More importantly, did we lose the sense of control or just an illusion of it? Reflecting on this question might put some things in perspective and help gain a different outlook on the power of moments.

One of the aspects of personality psychology is the concept of locus of control developed by Julian B. Rotter in 1954. According to his theory, people either have an external or internal locus of control. Externals believe that their life is governed by fate, destiny, and events outside of their immediate scope of control. Conversely, internals see themselves as the artisans of their own fortune. Logically, this would seem like a desirable trait for managers and high-profile business executives. However, in times of crisis, externals might find it easier to cope with unexpected change.

Although giving up on rigid long-term planning is recommended, it is not enough for leading a happy (and successful) life. You need to learn how to savor each day, one at a time. Yes, letting go is a legitimate skill. This does not mean that you should cease all efforts to develop and grow both professionally and personally. You do not need to know where you will be in x years, but you do need to establish patterns of behavior that will bring you closer to where you would like to eventually end up.

Achieving goals requires discipline and order. Sadly, setting goals is not a guarantee for what life has in store for you. The secret to success lies in finding an equilibrium between choosing one course and allowing yourself to joyfully go with the flow of life. Add this balancing act to your portfolio of skills to become a more valuable asset to your own business or to a company that merits you.

Guideline 14—Key Takeaways
1. Do not attempt to plan where you will be in x number of years.
2. Learn to let go by adopting a flexible approach to life.
3. Live in the moment but do not get locked in it.
4. Do not take anything for granted.
5. Develop patterns of behavior that will bring you closer to your overall goals.

GUIDELINE 15

Define Your Life Non-Negotiables

ONE of the essential steps of preparing for a negotiation is compiling the list of demands. Demands are the requests that you bring to the negotiation table. They are those elements that fill up the negotiation frame. The borders of this frame are designated by the measurable target—the maximum and minimum that either takes you closer or further away from your overall objective (what you want to achieve in the negotiation). If you were to compare a negotiation to a board game, the demands would be your chips for trade. You give something to get something. The currency is value. The beauty of the matter is that value is in the eye of the beholder.

Logically, you first want to trade the demands that have less worth to you. To do so, you need to place your demands in order of importance. The top-of-the-list ones are your non-negotiables. As the name itself suggests, you should not sacrifice these even if it means that you will have to walk away from the negotiation table. Never negotiate down with yourself. Convincing yourself in the heat of the negotiation that you can do without the things that are important to you will eventually backfire. It is only a matter of time. You will end up trying to find a way out of an agreement that does not feel satisfactory.

An executable and long-lasting agreement (be it with yourself or the other party) is the result of the acceptance of its perceived value. In the business environment, adding value has become the norm. The premium is creating value. That is what allows companies to excel over competition. Great organizations are made up of outstanding individuals. In the end, it all comes down to the human factor. Become a valuable resource, and you will never need to worry about lack of options.

The process of creating value should start from within. Define your life non-negotiables. What is the most important thing for *you*? For me, they are family and freedom. These two values drive my life choices. When we moved to the United States when I was a child, my parents told me that home is where the family is. This maxim brought a sense of comfort to our immigrant life. Since then, I have lived in many other countries, but in my heart, I always carried my home with me wherever I went. A solid internal foundation radiates to the outside world. It increases your bargaining power in all spheres of life. Genealogical roots have great potential for creating value.

I consider the monetary rewards of work as a way to provide a better life for my close ones. For me, money is about buying quality moments. This is the only thing that nobody can take away from us. The richer you are in memories, the stronger your remembering self becomes. In tough times, you can draw power from the good reminiscences.

My preference for freedom has always been my other non-negotiable. It is the lens through which I screen my employment opportunities and my career options. Work is a source of personal satisfaction for me, but it is gratifying only when I can perform it in an autonomous manner. This was one of the reasons behind the decision to quit my job at the law firm. Empowerment comes from setting goals and taking full responsibility for their execution. Although I initially paid a high price for my choice, the value it created in the long term was worth every penny.

In a way, my two top priorities create a system of interdependency. Without a solid foundation in the form of unwavering support from my family, I might not be as prone to taking on life's challenges. Independence comes from having a secure base. Once you figure out where your priorities are, you will notice that others will respect them too. Values are written on your face; a healthy system from within affects the whole ecosystem surrounding you. When it comes to defining the non-negotiables in your life, you can be selfish. Put on your own oxygen first before you help the person next to you.

Guideline 15—Key Takeaways
1. Make a list of your life demands.
2. Place the demands in order of importance.
3. Never negotiate down with yourself.
4. Respect your non-negotiables if you want others to acknowledge them.
5. Create value by setting your priorities.

GUIDELINE 16

Project the Outcome
You Want

SOME time ago, I was involved in moderating an intense negotiation session. Two business moguls, one from the hospitality industry and the other from the real estate sector, were discussing the terms of a rental agreement for several of their premises. Both sides were skilled negotiators. Consequently, each came well prepared and with clear expectations for how they would like the process to unfold to their best interests.

The real estate representative took the steer by presenting his extensive list of demands. His negotiator partner did not fall far behind. The negotiation started to resemble positional bargaining more than a principled negotiation where both parties strive to find a mutually acceptable solution. Neither wanted to make concessions, and each was stuck in their rigid positions. They were walking on a tightrope between an impasse and a deal.

What followed was one of the most brilliant tactics I have witnessed. Seeing that both parties were stubbornly defending their positions, the real estate party walked up to a flipchart standing in the middle of the meeting room. He explained that he was aware that his demands might be a bit confusing, therefore, he would organize them visually. He then proceeded to write down his demands point by point. What a genius psychological move.

He then sat back down at the table and continued the discussion where they had left it off. The negotiations went on all day, with a lunch break in between. All the while, the requests were in full sight. The real estate representative spent less energy on defending them. Nonetheless, the meeting ended with 80 percent of his written down demands accepted by the other party. The exact same demands that were at first fiercely rejected by the other party gracefully found their way into the final agreement.

The written word holds miraculous powers. For some reason, ink on paper is associated with legitimacy. If it is written down, it is imprinted on the mind. Perhaps this is due to the fact that many people's mental imagery is prevailingly visual. Consequently, what one sees, one is unconsciously primed to eventually accept. You just need to look at it long enough. Visualization, therefore, is a powerful technique. Use it to achieve the goals you set in your life negotiations. Project the future outcome that you want by displaying it on a vision board.

The Visualization-Confidence-Realization (VCR) technique mentioned earlier had a retrospective outlook; vision boards (also called dream or mood boards) are future-oriented. They consist of a collage of pictures, images, quotes, and other visual representations of one's dreams. Their aim is to serve as a directional source of motivation.

Here are a few tips on how to create them. First of all, be very specific about what you want to achieve. Set a timeframe for the realization of your goals. Limit the number of words you put on the board to one sentence; rely on imagery instead. Make the projection statement simple and precise, for example: **By [input date], I will achieve [insert what you want].** Please notice the wording used: I *will*. Such phrasing does not allow a failure option. The "I will" formula is a self-non-negotiable. Avoid weak energy phrases such as: I would like to, I hope for, I should, if only I could, it would be nice to have, and so on.

Approach the board design like a brainstorming session—do not limit yourself and allow your dreams to flow freely. Restrain yourself from criticizing them and do not allow doubt concerning their realization to creep in. In this moment, there is no need to negotiate down with yourself. The sky is the limit when it comes to your dreams!

Add your own photos next to the pictures and images you paste on the board. If you want a house, for example, find an image that most closely resembles the type of residence you dream of living in. Then put your picture inside of that house. Create anticipatory emotions—imagine how it would feel if you were already in your dream home. Where would you be right now, how would it make you feel, and so on.

When you are finished with your visionary design, place the board somewhere you can see it every day. A bedroom is a good place because it will be the last thing you see each night before you close your eyes and the first thing you wake up tc. Let it be the frame of your day.

Last but not least, it is not enough to cut out images and paste them on the board. Now that you have a global view of what you want, it is time to manifest it to reality. Your mind is already primed; now it is time for the body to follow. Take small actions every single day that will bring you closer to your desired goals. Tick off the things you manage to achieve. This will be an incentive to close up the whole dream list. Do not forget to reward yourself for every little achievement.

Guideline 16—Key Takeaways
1. Use visualization to achieve the goals you set in your life negotiations.
2. Project the future you want by displaying it on a vision board.
3. Use this formula: "By [input date], I will achieve [insert what you want]."
4. Create anticipatory emotions by pasting your pictures next to your dreams.
5. Take necessary action to tick off the elements on your board.

Develop High-Performance Habits

THE two most productive habits that govern my adult life, reading and sports, were both developed when I was a child. I intentionally used the passive voice because both were embedded independently of my control, but within the scope of my choice, which was a critical success factor. My parents and I moved to the United States when I was almost seven years old. At that age, and under the right conditions, it is relatively easy to inflict new behavior patterns. I started attending school as soon as we settled in, although I did not know any English. That was quite a bold experiment on my parent's part. Perhaps that too became a habit because my life since then follows that same pattern.

I clearly recall the moment I developed a passion for reading. Our reasoning skills teacher had an unconventional approach to education. She removed the mandatory textbook and course reading list from the syllabus. Instead, we were asked to read at least one book per month. The novel element was that we could select whatever work interested us. Additional class time was allocated for discovering the extensive library collections at our own pace. To this day, a library or bookshop is a comforting place for me because it brings back memories of a carefree and non-imposed time. Thanks to that teacher, reading became not only an enriching mental escape but also a high-return investment for me.

The existence of choice is the ultimate form of freedom for the one who has it and a powerful tool of motivation for the one who grants it. Consequently, desirable habits can be instilled by proper setting and allowing for the liberty to choose, even if it relates to what you want to read. It also requires an understanding of the preferences and natural inclinations of the individual. To find out what yours are, you may need to experiment a bit. For example, I engaged in many sports activities throughout my life to narrow down my physical activity to a few selected forms that I like. Enjoyment is a critical component of ingraining a habit.

Negotiations are often classified as one of the more emotionally charged human interactions. In stressful circumstances, it is recommended to have a pre-determined pattern of behavior that limits the reliance on emotions. Under danger or attack, it is then easier to go in auto-pilot mode if a habitual behavior pre-exists. For example, an army is trained for the unexpected by rehearsed drills. High-performance negotiators need to have a habitual pattern of behavior as a fallback position in case negotiations get tough. Since it takes anywhere between 18 to 254 days to develop a habit, it is worth getting started before the actual need for high-performance arises.

In the course of my work with business professionals, I have identified four key characteristics of high-impact negotiators. The findings are as follows: emotional stability, a proactive approach, a multi dimensional outlook, and positive energy. Emotionally stable negotiators can withstand difficult situations and handle setbacks, all the while remaining efficient in the process. They are governed by reason and logic rather than by emotions. Many sport disciplines require self-management and overcoming of personal limitations. Sport also teaches proactiveness, which is understood as the ability to make decisions and execute them in order to reach a specific goal.

A multi dimensional outlook is a result of cultivating interdisciplinary interests. Negotiations call for a broad array of skills. Success comes much easier to those who master communication and interpersonal skills, the art of persuasion, the basics of psychology, perception and impression management techniques, and elements of intercultural sensitivity. Reading is the best way to expand mental horizons. Follow the Buffet Formula "Go to bed smarter than when you woke up" and develop the habit of reading before nighttime.

Positive energy can offset the tension of a stressful negotiation. Its benefits are dual—for yourself and the other party. It is often the cheapest concession that you can make. Negotiation is a mirror. What you display in terms of self-assurance and attitude is reflected in the actions of your partner and ultimately affects their behavior toward you. Positive energy is contagious. Be the one who spreads it around.

Sport is the best natural mood stimulator. During exercise, regardless of its type, the body releases endorphins. These chemicals work in a similar way to drugs called opioics, which relieve pain and lead to euphoria. The feeling they produce is similar to the action of morphine. The only difference is that it is legal.

High performance and healthy habits seem to be positively correlated. Success in negotiations is often the result of practices established outside of the negotiation zone. A habit is a three-step process that consists of the cue (for example, feeling stressed), the routine (for example, going for a walk), and the reward (feeling less anxiety). It all starts with a properly framed incentive. Any habitual behavior can be altered, provided the cue and the reward stay more or less the same. To break an old habit, you need to replace the old routine with a new one of your preference. Why not choose an activity that will enhance your overall performance and bring you closer to achieving your projected future?

Guideline 17—Key Takeaways
1. Develop healthy habits as early as possible.
2. Instill good habits by proper scene-setting.
3. Exercise the freedom to choose the (good) habit that you want to develop.
4. Ingrain a (good) habit by introducing the element of enjoyment.
5. Cultivate activities that develop emotional stability, require a proactive approach and multi dimensional outlook, and stimulate positive energy.

GUIDELINE 18

Frequent the Best Places

As far back as I can remember, my parents ingrained the habit of work in me. When I wanted to get pocket money when I was a child, I needed to do small chores around the house. With time, those little tasks evolved to larger and more serious ones as I took on more responsibilities, such as helping out in my parents' business throughout my summer breaks. This taught me the relation between labor and money. It was natural for me that rewards were attributed on the basis of invested effort. It was gratifying to have my own financial means and the sense of liberty that they gave.

That attitude partially got me through my academic studies. When I got my Socrates Erasmus scholarship at the law faculty during my Masters, I chose to study in one of the nicer places—in Nice in the South of France. The grant covered student housing, catering in the canteen (an unforgettable culinary experience), and a modest budget for the fun side of the student experience. The latter covered going out (maximum twice a month) and hunting for the best take-out deals. The competition was strong in that department. Anything left on the windowsill, which served as a personal fridge (we were sharing one per three other rooms) was consumed by giant seagulls. They were more streetwise than me.

The French Riviera is a haven of material abundance and the ultimate high life. The azure coast is lined with the most splendid hotels with their private beach clubs, luxury yachts sway in the turquoise sea, sports cars roar down the Promenade des Anglais and high-fashion boutiques showcase the latest fashion trends. Few are immune to this sensory, albeit materialistic, wonderland. Window shopping and daydreaming were among my favorite pastimes, because the only thing that I had an abundance of back then was time.

Naturally, I wanted to get a taste of the glamorous life. Yet again, my parents used my student dream as an incentive for me to work harder.

Once per semester, provided I got a high enough total score in the exam session, my reward arrived. When the results came, I would get a wire transfer for the equivalent of a fancy four-course luncheon at one of the most luxurious establishments on the Promenade des Anglais.

What a treat that was! I savored every moment of this unforgettable experience. It was not just about the exquisite food, but the manner in which it was served and how unique being in that five-star setting made you feel. The service was impeccable, and the surroundings were grandiose. For the time of the meal, one was transported into a different world. A taste of the good life leaves one craving for more.

When you find yourself in any given surroundings, you expose yourself to an array of visual stimuli. For example, when you go to a five-star restaurant, the mind registers the fancy décor, the attention to every detail in the interior design, the fine silverware, the opulent fragrances, the savory dishes, and the elegant people you encounter. Did you ever notice how differently people behave in such places? They usually bring their best attire and manners to the table, speak in a more sophisticated way, and sit up straight. The *luxury effect* lasts longer than the meal. If cultivated, it may turn into a permanent mood that will affect other spheres of life.

Our environment strongly impacts how we perceive and how we feel about ourselves. If you frequent the best places, you will feel like a better version of yourself. Even one artificially created moment can leave a lasting impression and impact your future preferences by introducing specific standards. After all, life is nothing more than a collage of moments. On the subconscious level, exposure to one stimulus (the luxury setting, for example) influences your actions and responses to subsequent stimuli. In psychology, this phenomenon is called priming. Priming is perceptual; it can be either positive or negative.

I partially agree with what Brian Tracy said: "You cannot control what happens to you, but you can control your attitude toward what happens to you, and in that, you will be mastering change rather than allowing it to master you." Certainly, we cannot fully control what happens to us. However, we can partially influence events by priming ourselves for the positive. It can be achieved through deliberate exposure to pleasant external stimuli. This experience will create an optimistic mindset and energy.

Happy vibes are like a magnet for attracting people. By positive stimulation, you also invite good things to your life. Some refer to this as manifesting. Start the cycle by treating yourself to the finer things in life, in whichever form you wish: a fancy meal, a hike in beautiful scenery, or a trip to your dream destination. The best places bring out the best in you. Work hard to then pamper yourself with what makes you feel splendid.

Guideline 18—Key Takeaways
1. Reward yourself for your efforts.
2. Get a taste of the good life.
3. Go to the best places to soak up the atmosphere.
4. Expose yourself to positive stimuli (people, events, places, nature).
5. Prime yourself for success.

GUIDELINE 19

Build an Aura of Desirability

THE biggest disadvantage of moments of bliss is the hard landing back to reality. This is a short-term inconvenience, a blessing in disguise, actually. Overcoming the momentary discomfort will prove beneficial in the long run. It is difficult to lower standards once they have been elevated. Loss aversion, especially when the deprivation relates to something pleasant, is a strong motivator. That is why it pays off to treat oneself to something extraordinary once in a while. Superior quality is an investment. With time and directional effort, the one-off events will occur more often. The goal is for high standards to become the norm, both in business and beyond.

Negotiating is not the same as selling. To persuade at the moment you need something is a moment too late. Consequently, desirability has to be crafted in advance. You have to set specific standards and prime your negotiation partner for accepting them on the unconscious level first. People are self-aware and cautious once the negotiation officially starts. They are more prone to mental priming outside of the perceived negotiation zone. Double standards create a cognitive dissonance that most people would prefer to avoid. If you have high standards outside the negotiation, others will naturally anticipate the same when the interaction begins.

Have you ever wondered what differentiates winners from all the other players? Even when new technologies, services, or products (such as vaccines, for example) are introduced, the novelty effect wears off very quickly, and competition steps in. It is difficult to stay on the podium unless you can operate on a higher—perceptual and emotional—level. Winners know that customers do not buy a product or service, but rather emotions. A vaccine buys peace of mind, a car grants freedom, prestige, and so on. Build an aura of desirability around yourself (your company, products, or services), and you will never be short on offers.

Desire is a sublime concept. Consequently, mental stimulation requires attention to each and every single element. The devil is in the details, as the saying goes. This is one of the (few good) things I learned at the law firm. I vividly recall one situation when the managing partner called for an early morning meeting. A group of lawyers, including myself, had been preparing a complex contract for one of our clients. We were working against a short deadline, and neither of us had gotten much sleep for the past few days. All our energy was channeled on closing the legal loopholes and making sure there would be no exposure for the client. The document we submitted the night before was bulletproof in terms of its content.

We were exhausted, but we happily gathered around the vast meeting room, hoping for some praise following all the hard work. The centerpiece of the room was a mahogany table that gave justice to the joke about size compensating for a lack in other departments. The managing partner walked in, and without a word, threw a handful of contracts on the table. They glided across the polished surface, some falling to the floor. There must have been around fifty documents in total. "You have exactly thirty seconds to find our contract," he threw our way. This particular deadline we did not manage to meet.

The theatrical gesture was his way of teaching us a lesson about quality and high standards. He wanted the contracts that left his firm to be easily distinguishable from the documents issued by all of his competitors. They were to have the letterhead, proper formatting and page setting, a specific quality of print paper, font size and type, and ink color. He knew that he could not compete solely by selling expertise and content. The other law firms were already doing that. His trademark was a prestigious advisory service, which had its reflection in the hefty legal fees.

Perfectionism and attention to detail are critical factors in creating an aura of uniqueness and desirability. It is the experience that counts, not necessarily the product or service offering. The latter can and most likely will be forgotten, but impressions will stay. Adequate quality is a given. A touch of luxury (in whichever form) is what makes the difference. High personal and professional standards seldom go unnoticed. They need to be crafted before you need to rely on their powers.

Guideline 19—Key Takeaways
1. Invest in superior quality.
2. Make high standards become the norm for yourself.
3. Prime your negotiation partner before making an offer.
4. Pay attention to details.
5. Create your own and unique brand, then make it an object of desire.

GUIDELINE 20

Dress for Success

IMPRESSION management is the process of exercising influence over the perception that people have regarding a person, situation, or object. This definition may suggest that impression management is outward-oriented—toward other people. Contrary to common understanding, impression management should initially be a reverse, inward-focused activity. Preparation for a negotiation starts with self-composition on the emotional and ego-tional level. The same principle applies to impression management. "A well-tied tie is the first serious step in life" (Oscar Wilde).

Forget the cliché about first impressions. We all know how they work and that it takes a split-second to form a first impression. Most of us have also been sensitized to the dangers of first impression errors, especially in an intercultural organizational setting. The focus should switch to self-impression, because this is where the process really starts. A positive first impression is difficult to make if you do not feel good about yourself.

The English proverb says, "Clothes don't make the man," but they certainly impact how one feels. Well-being is the starting point of any successful endeavor. Job and academic titles have magical powers; that is why you should strive to get the best one. Notice what happens when someone refers to you by your professional identity. You start acting the part. A professor should be knowledgeable and rational. A business executive should be agile, dynamic, and task-oriented. A negotiator should be flexible, open-minded, and smart. The label drives the behavior. Clothes labels have the same effect. Dress the part to become the part.

Few people are immune to signs of authority. Socialization has taught us to regard uniforms as symbols of a certain status. In consequence, a particular costume triggers a behavioral autopilot reaction. Disguise can be a powerful tool of manipulation. For example, experiments have shown that a person garmented as a doctor will have much higher response rates to questions about intimate matters than the same person less the professional attire. The outfit has become an insignia of power. It is a pre-requisite to achieving the goals you set out for yourself.

Do not wait until you are successful to start looking it. Dress as if you are already in the position you want to have. Observe what is the dress code in the professional environment you want to enter, then copy the overall flavor. One of the core principles of negotiation is similarity. If you look like one of them, they will treat you like their own. Of course, this can also be used to make an adverse impression, should your goal be to stand out and distance yourself from the other party.

Appropriate attire should fit your personality and individual style. Even if you mimic an environmental dress code, it is recommended you personalize it to suit your preferences. What you wear has to feel comfortable and empowering. The aim is for it to camouflage your mental insecurities and inner doubts. Notice how differently you feel when you dress up. You can manipulate your self-image to feel more in control (fake it till you make it). Remember that power comes from within and radiates externally. Others will regard you the way that you carry yourself.

Dressing for success does not refer to garments only. Your Curriculum Vitae and your professional social networks also deserve proper attire. They, too, are subject to impression management. On the internal level, they often fall victim to the downgrading of individual achievements, as I have noticed in my business and academic practice. Modesty is a virtue, but apply it with moderation when you craft your CV.

Your resumé should start with a strong, concise, and professional profile that includes a few lines or bullet points about who you are. It should precede the enlisting of your education and professional experience. Those first few lines of your CV are the equivalent of a first impression; you do not want to mess it up externally. Internally, the profile description will reinforce you and make you act the part. It is recommended to gather a few opinions about yourself from your network to see how others perceive you, then make a condensed summary of the main strong points you collected. Others will be better suited to perform this exercise because they are more objective and less critical in their views than you would be about yourself.

If you exist on social media, be very careful what you post about yourself. The Internet never forgets. Pay particular attention to the title you choose for yourself on professional network sites. Avoid vague profile descriptions, such as "future psychologist," "looking for new opportunities," "open to new offers." The latter two send a clear signal— I have nothing else going on for me at the moment. Desirability is a herd instinct; people want what others want (and often, what they cannot easily have or access). There is nothing wrong with looking for new opportunities. In fact, it should be a perpetual process. Lack of options does not look good on anyone.

Guideline 20—Key Takeaways
1. Focus on self-impression before you attempt to manage external impressions.
2. Dress the part to become the part.
3. Do not wait until you are successful to start looking like it.
4. Let dress be your armor—it serves as camouflage for your mental insecurities and inner doubts.
5. Design a strong, concise, and professional profile (a few lines at the beginning of your CV and as a title on your professional social media).

GUIDELINE 21

Life Is a Journey (Aka the Airplane Test)

YOU might be familiar with the informal candidate selection tool referred to as the airplane test. The logic of this assessment is straightforward: would you like to spend several hours with this person as your co-passenger on a flight, and would you feel comfortable having them as the representative of your company? The test adds the aspect of likeability to the standard package that consists of job qualifications, KSAs (knowledge, skills, and abilities), and WRCs (work-related characteristics). It broadens the selection criteria by the human factor. Do you need any more proof that business is personal?

In some aspects, the airplane test is similar to the elevator pitch—a condensed synopsis of who you are, what you do, and what you are looking to do. The latter should be short and sweet. Its aim is to present yourself and your business experience in a compelling and memorable manner. As the name itself suggests, your auto-presentation should not take longer than an elevator ride would (the concept came to life in a skyscraper type of environment). The two often go hand-in-hand, sometimes in the literal sense. You never know when you might be making an elevator pitch during a flight …

Have you ever switched jobs on a plane? I have, although it took me several years to realize it. During my dual professional life split between the workweek in Paris, France and weekend lectures in Poland, the two airports became my second home. I knew some of the flight attendants who were operating the standard Friday-Sunday flights by name. The crew members and I exchanged local gossip and goodies from both destinations. On my lucky days, they treated me to a courtesy upgrade. I was welcomed on board in a manner that caught the attention of the other passengers. Some even thought that I was famous. Illusory fame is sufficient to attract more people. During that exotic travel schedule, I made at least as many business connections as air miles. One turned out to be life-altering.

My plans for the travel time were always ambitious. On the way to the lectures, I would have a stack of student papers to review. Coming back, I usually had a few presentations that needed to be perfected for the upcoming week. Seldom did I get a chance to realize my plans and finalize all my work on the plane. What usually happened was that the person sitting next to me and I would strike up a conversation. It was then that I learned that deadlines and tasks are negatively correlated—the less time you have, the more tasks you can efficiently condense in a limited timeframe. If you want something done, give it to a busy person.

I distinctly remember one such arm-to-arm flight conversation. The person who was sitting next to me was a retired professor from Switzerland. He was flying from Paris to visit his relatives in Poland over the weekend. It turned out that we were born in the same city and that we were both academics. The similarity principle is one of the fundamental ones in negotiation and beyond. Despite the age gap, we found many similarities between us. Somewhere above the clouds, a thread of understanding was created. This bond grew stronger over the years during which we kept in touch on a pen-pal basis.

It was not until several years after that memorable flight that I realized that I had successfully completed the airplane test. As time passed, my business activities expanded, and I was working out of Paris all over Europe. The lifestyle of constant travel was starting to weigh heavy on me. I needed a change. It came in the form of an offer from the professor to establish an inter-institutional cooperation between our universities. The activities would be managed from an academic unit in Switzerland. For me, this was a chance to settle down in one place where I could bridge my business practice with academic acumen. Another big move, this time to the land of chocolate, cheese, and watches, was on the horizon.

The airplane test knows neither the day nor the hour. Its greatest advantage is that it is based on authenticity, both in real life and in the interview process. You cannot anticipate who you will meet and how that random encounter might change the course of your life. Keep your eyes open for new opportunities. You might make the outcome of the journey more interesting if you elevate your standards. Chances are that others will perceive and treat you accordingly. An upgrade, in whichever form you find fit, is an investment in your image, network pool, and future opportunities.

Guideline 21—Key Takeaways
1. Increase your likeability factor.
2. Have your elevator pitch ready—who you are, what you do, and what you are looking to do.
3. Travel light—free of negative emotional baggage.
4. Be open to networking opportunities wherever life takes you.
5. Upgrade to personal business class.

GUIDELINE 22

Communicate Like a Boss

ACCORDING to research, ineffective communication skills account for over 80 percent of managerial failure. The intriguing question is to which extent does the inability to accurately communicate impair reaching managerial heights. The communication process is self-revelatory. The way a person expresses themselves, the types of words they use, and what they talk about reveals their social and professional status, education, life experiences, cultural background, state of mind, and so on. That is why one of the classic open interview questions is, "Tell us about yourself." How they hear you is how they perceive you.

Be careful to avoid the phenomenon referred to as the misrepresentation effect. It occurs because people rarely communicate anything without a specific, consciously or unconsciously pre-determined, plan in mind. Their aim is to make a particular effect, be it for other people to agree with them, perceive them in a specific way, or give them what they want. As a result, both communicators focus more on effect-management than on truly understanding each other. Special effects may be engaging in the movies, but they are strenuous in real life. Sometimes it is refreshing to let the masks come off.

The misrepresentation effect, along with the fact that people are imperfect communicators, causes many negotiations to go astray. When entering a negotiation, it is helpful to keep in mind that the communication process very seldom is a pure, neutral, and objective one. People do not willingly disclose all the information in their possession. They either deliberately withhold bits of it for their advantage, or they unintentionally do not display all the knowledge that they hold. Furthermore, each party might have different interests and their ideas on how they should be satisfied. Accordingly, how we communicate our goals is tainted by what we actually want to achieve. The end goal determines how we communicate.

There are various techniques for avoiding the misrepresentation effect and improving the communication process with the aim of grasping the hidden message and discovering the real intentions of the other party. When it comes to communicating, the old proverb, "Silence is golden" seems to enter a new dimension. The first rule of any process that requires obtaining information from the other party is allowing them to talk. This should be fairly simple. People have an enormous need for expressing themselves and being heard. The tricky part is the ability to truly listen.

Emotional exhibitionism seems to be a sign of our times, an observation which is reflected in the term selfie generation that was introduced in my book *Negotiation Booster: The Ultimate Self-Empowerment Guide to High-Impact Negotiations*. The various online social networks and information exchange portals serve as a vent for communicating and freeing the ego. Ironically, the heavy overload of correspondence makes people more immune to what others are really saying. The constant information flow lessens our perception of what is being conveyed in the heart of the message. In consequence, we are steadily losing the ability to listen, both in private and professional surroundings. Those who possess this skill are like diamonds in the rough. The capacity to actively listen is by far the most desired characteristic of a master negotiator.

Negotiation should be a process of hearing rather than talking, a balancing act between reason and emotions. It is an art of self-management. By applying reasoning to what we hear, we can manage our perception and rein in feelings that the speaker may evoke in us. It is at times a counterintuitive process. For example, when in the best interests of the negotiation we force ourselves to restrain from succumbing to negative feelings caused by the other party or avoid striking back just to flex our bargaining muscle.

While it is essential to maintain an objective stance, it is also recommended to listen with the use of emotions. Pay particular attention to the choice of words of the speaker. They designate what is considered reality from the point of view of the other person. Words are a valuable source of information about the speaker and their needs. Figuring out what is essential for the other party and presenting yourself (your proposal, CV, or service offering) as the answer to their wants are critical steps in establishing an interpersonal bond.

Some of my consulting mandates included screening job applications, specifically reviewing candidates' motivation letters. I noticed that the majority of them were written from the "I" perspective: I want to work for your firm, I want to learn new skills, I want to join the best … basically me, myself, and I. A well-rounded motivation letter should not only explain the reasons why you are applying for a specific position. More importantly, it should answer one fundamental question: if you hire me, how will I be of assistance to *you*. The letter should, therefore, be crafted from the self-interest perspective of the company and not yours. It should address the question: What is in it for the other party? Remember that words create impressions. "They may forget what you said — but they will never forget how you made them feel" (Carl W. Buehner). In this sense, words can be used as a tool of psychological influence.

Listening should not be limited to the physical act of hearing what is being verbally expressed. Non-verbal and para-verbal communication forms an integral part of the negotiation process. While you actively listen to the words, watch out for changes in body language and take note of the manner in which things are said (para-verbals). A skilled negotiator should thus operate on all three levels of communication: verbal, non-verbal, and para-verbal.

Furthermore, negotiation is a process of information gathering and uncovering the ego. A savvy communicator aims at collecting multidimensional information: both explicit and implicit. Listen beyond the words. Register all the features that characterize the other person. Pay particular attention to the attributes of their professional and social status and look for glimpses of the ego reflected in attire, gadgets, jewelry, cars, office design, job titles, and so on. The ego lies in the details. These small indicators form the overall image of the other party. They help to figure out what makes the other person *click* and what might be the individual's hot buttons or weaknesses.

In order to obtain exhaustive information, it is recommended to pose open questions. An example of an open question may be: What would have to be modified for you to accept this agreement? What are you looking for in an ideal job candidate? What does it take to succeed in this job? Some interviewees erroneously assume that it is not their role to ask questions. By failing to do so, they automatically place themselves in a submissive, reactive position. If you want others to treat you like a boss, you need to express yourself like one.

Guideline 22—Key Takeaways
1. Beware of the misrepresentation effect.
2. Develop the ability to listen effectively.
3. Listen beyond the words.
4. Look for signs of the ego and feed it.
5. Communicate like a boss without being bossy.

GUIDELINE 23

Be Selective

THE result of a job interview is pretty much a zero-sum game. You are either hired, immediately or at a later time when a future opportunity in the same firm opens up, or you are rejected. Those who find themselves in the latter group seldom get the chance to learn the exact reasons behind the negative decision. What happens behind closed doors is referred to as selection. It is the process of collecting and evaluating information about the work-related characteristics (WRCs), the knowledge, skills, and abilities (KSAs) referred to as competencies, and the personality type of a potential job candidate.

Smart companies make selection decisions with a great deal of care and control over the number of applicants, the information they gather, and its assessment. They are well aware that from an organizational perspective, matching the candidate's profile to the job requirements leads to the achievement of corporate objectives, an optimal allocation of resources, competitive advantage, and an overall stronger company. Follow their example.

A few months after the octopus drawing interview adventure, the HR manager of the business school invited me back for a meeting related to another job opportunity. This time the interview did not include any sketching activities. Therefore, it went much better. It was clear that the interviewer believed I had the competencies necessary for the job. I was optimistic that this time I would land the job. Much to my surprise, the HR manager called me with bad news. They chose another candidate for the role. Since we had established trust, he was open with me when I asked for the reason behind the decision. He said: "We already had a similar personality type in the team. We wanted to change the dynamic by bringing in someone with different personality traits."

Work-related characteristics and competencies alone are not sufficient to succeed in job negotiations. The right personality mosaic is equally important. People spend a lot of their time, effort, money, and energy on elevating their skillset portfolio. What about the development of personality? I am often asked in conferences whether a good negotiator is born or made. The great news is that we were all once the best negotiators. For a baby, it is sufficient to cry to have at least one person tending to their needs. Negotiation ability (the physical capacity alone) does not translate into elevated negotiation skills.

Some people are naturally cabled to negotiate more efficiently. They have favorable predispositions in terms of certain inherited traits, such as higher emotional intelligence (EQ), an elevated cognitive ability (IQ), and self-monitoring, defined as the ability to recognize the impact of our behavior. Facets of negotiation can be acquired through proper training, practice, and implementation. A good negotiator is someone who combines nature and nurture.

This brings us to the concept of personality formation. According to research, personality consists of heredity (50–55 percent) and environment (the rest). One cannot (as yet) fully impact the genetic code. Some of the external factors can be controlled and modified. The environment consists of the initial socio-economic level—family, as well as other group membership, and overall life experiences. Some theories conclude that personality is the end result of the three people you most often associate with. Who you spend time with is who you become. This is rather obvious on a personal level. It should be no different on the professional front.

Therefore, be very selective about which companies you agree to work with and for. Their organizational culture will rub off on you, and eventually, it will impact your mental wiring. Your career track is like your professional ID card. Other people will make judgments about you based on the league you are in. I have seen many candidates from renowned firms breeze through the recruitment process on the wings of the brand of their former employers.

If companies are highly selective, so should you be about where you choose to invest your time once you accept an offer. Your personal return on investment (PROI) is an efficiency assessment tool that measures the ratio between profit and costs. On the personal investment level, it consists of hygiene and motivator factors. The former are remuneration and work conditions; this is the standard package (which does not mean that the conditions you negotiate should be average). Motivator factors are development and growth opportunities, expansion of skills, advancement possibilities, networking perspectives—all the aspects that will enrich your personality and yield a higher PROI.

Invest your job search time wisely. I often hear job candidates complain that they have sent out a hundred CVs to no avail. The problem is that they submitted exactly the same document to all the companies. Your CV needs to be tailored and adjusted to the firm you are targeting. Sometimes it is just a matter of rewording and adding a few buzz words that are used in the job opening or appear on the company website (the mission statement is a good reference point). Refrain from submitting your application for the sake of applying—if you do not meet the job criteria or are not fully convinced you are interested in the work. It is a small world. Soon enough your application might surface and be labeled as the CV spammer in the recruiter circle.

When presented with a job offer(s), make sure you are crystal clear about why you are accepting it. Consider how acceptance will impact your future prospects beyond the satisfaction of the hygiene factors. After all, you will be spending the majority of your life at work. You want it to be quality time. Make sure that the job will lead to the achievement of your professional objectives, an optimal allocation of your personal resources, that it will bring you a competitive advantage should you choose to move on, and that it will enrich your personality. Being selective will allow you to better align your personality characteristics with the job. This is the ultimate recipe for a work-life fit.

Guideline 23—Key Takeaways
1. Develop your personality in parallel to growing your skillset.
2. Be choosy about who you associate with on a personal and professional level.
3. Perform a personal return on investment (PROI) analysis before you accept a job offer.
4. Structure your job search in an efficient manner.
5. Make sure that the job fulfills your objectives and serves as a springboard for success and further growth.

GUIDELINE 24

Build Trust

Do you recall the airplane test? Many years after I met the retired professor on the plane, he reached out with an idea to establish an inter-institutional cooperation between the two European universities we were working for. That is how I ended up moving from Paris to Switzerland. There is a saying among the Swiss regarding the flow of time, "If you want to age slower, move to Switzerland." The academic curriculum felt like a breeze compared to the balancing act between my weekday manager and weekend lecturer role.

Old habits die hard. I never followed a singular path, neither at university nor in my professional life. It felt strange wearing only one hat, as if the time train had passed and I was left behind on the empty station. I needed something more to fill up my schedule. My quest for additional activities eventually bore fruit. I was offered a part-time position at the United Nations (UN) in Geneva.

When I first took on the role, my idea was that the consulting activities would be strictly technical. After all, the title of Senior Adviser for Multi-stakeholder Engagement obliges, or so I thought. Much to my surprise, most of the work was related to providing assistance in building trust among the multi-party actors at the UN level. It is there that I understood how important this elusive concept is for securing long-term and lasting interactions.

Collaboration requires trust. Trust is what allows people to enter into a relationship in spite of uncertainty or lack of complete clarity and certitude. Is this not the definition of life? Trust is a pre-requisite of every system, be it professional or personal. Trust increases the feeling of security between parties. Without it, the relation would be governed by fear and would require constant control. Trust, therefore, has an economic value.

Building trust is a step-by-step process. It results from working together and is then strengthened by experiences of reliable interactions. Mistrust is not an enemy of trust; it is the natural component on the way to paving trust. The secret lies in how the layers of mistrust are slowly lifted. It all starts at the interview phase when the two parties come together for the first time. Their above-the-waterline, visible and explicit objective is to close a business transaction. To a large extent, their success will depend on whether they can establish a thread of trust at the outset. The fundamental question that any recruiter silently asks themselves is, "Can I trust this person?" The same query should be mirrored in the mind of the candidate before they make their decision. Trust is a two-way street.

I recently got a call from a work colleague from whom I had not heard for many years. We used to work together right after I moved to Switzerland. We never really got to know each other since shortly after I joined, she left for another job. She was calling me with an offer to take over a slice of her business activities while she would be away on a mission for a few months. I was not convinced. The proposal itself was interesting enough, but something felt off.

During the call, she was making derogatory references to the institution we first met at. She was trying to paint a favorable picture of the other unit by comparing it to the previous work environment. There is nothing wrong with some good old selling tactics. In fact, it is only natural that during the job interview or negotiation, both parties want to present their offering in the best light. However, one should be careful not to badmouth past employers. Discretion is an honorable trait. Lack thereof in one situation allows one to suspect that the person might cause offense to confidential information in different circumstances. If you are ever asked why you left your former employer, simply say that you moved on to explore other business horizons, which is, in fact, what you are doing. Do not defame; it will only backfire.

Trust takes time and working together. Like any construction, it starts with the first brick. At the beginning of the relationship, your role is to present yourself as a person who has the fundamental characteristics of a trustworthy individual, such as professional and personal competence, reliability, integrity, honesty and openness, a caring and respectful attitude, as well as integrity. The latter means that you walk the talk. Once you enter the relation, you will need to provide proof by displaying behaviors that serve as testimony. Trust is fragile, so handle it with care. It takes a lot to establish trust, but one moment can destroy it.

One of the conditions of longevity in business relationships is the capacity to achieve a balance between the task and relationship. This is a fine line. In a job negotiation, you want to secure employment options that will tick off your list of demands to the greatest extent possible. However, you might not be offered a job if you do not *click* with the person with whom you are interacting. One of the click conditions is the budding possibility of establishing trust.

When I first moved to Switzerland, one of the things I was astounded by was the lack of formality of employment documents. My work agreements were fairly basic and straightforward. The provisions usually fit on one page and covered the job title, tasks and responsibilities, remuneration, work time, and a few other conditions. Simplicity, at least in relation to labor contracts, became the norm for me.

That is why I did not react well when I received a request for a training back in Poland for one of the big multinational hubs there. The standard negotiations for this assignment came to a sudden impasse once I received the contract for the training. It was 37 pages long! The detailed review of all the legal clauses would take longer than the two training days that it was drafted for. I recall that my first impression was that this firm does not trust me for some reason. This perception then adversely affected my attitude toward the person in charge of the training. In the end, we managed to overcome the legal hassle, but the training was not the most enjoyable experience for me.

Trust is not in opposition to contracts and other formal arrangements. In fact, contracts require trust in order to be signed, and then they strengthen the trust provided the terms are respected and implemented. However, haggling too much over the task-oriented details may fog your vision when it comes to the relation. It is recommended to separate the task from the relationship. If you can have someone negotiate the terms of your engagement for you, step out of the picture.

Guideline 24—Key Takeaways
1. Establish a thread of trust at the beginning of the relationship.
2. Work together with the other party to establish trust and strengthen it by reliable interactions.
3. Build the characteristics of a trustworthy individual: professional and personal competence, reliability, integrity, honesty and openness, a caring and respectful attitude, and integrity.
4. Take care not to ruin the trust.
5. Separate the task from the relationship.

GUIDELINE 25

Momentum Is Everything

DECISION making is problematic because it changes the *status quo*. Contrary to common belief, people do not fear change itself, but rather the unknown related to introducing a new order. That is why change management is such a popular topic both in organizational settings and in business schools. Success in life depends, among others, on swift decision making. The same moment will never occur twice; therefore, you need to go for it before it is gone. Like my mentor once told me, "You can postpone decisions. Life will eventually make some of them for you. However, be ready to live with the consequences." I learned that he was right the hard way.

Change is inevitable; it is the only constant that you can safely bet on. One of the reasons why companies do not successfully implement change is because they do not allow their people to grieve. The transition period between the old and the new is a critical condition for harmony and the acceptance of novelty. Sitting on the fence between the two orders is natural, provided this does not become the favorite spot.

When the perspective of the move to Switzerland linked to the setting up of the inter-institutional cooperation appeared, I was more than ready for a change. Working between two countries, a crazy schedule with no days off, and weekly travel proved exhausting in the long run. In my mind's eye, I was longing for a more stable schedule and a calmer way of life.

The job interview went well. Consequently, I was offered a full-time position at the university almost immediately after the meeting. That is when something strange happened. When the moment came for me to make my decision, I suddenly did not want to let go of my existing set-up. The fatigue and suitcase life seemed more appealing than change itself. I hesitated in giving my reply and prolonged the negotiation process for as long as I could. I was hoping that with time, it would get easier to accept change.

The price I paid for that illusional luxury was very high. Once I finally made up my mind to accept the job, I was informed that the position I was initially offered was gone. Academic posts fill up fast, and there are not that many of them. New ones open infrequently. Eventually, I managed to secure another job at the same unit, but ... it took me three years to get to the level that I was first interviewed and selected for.

Hesitation is a result of the anxiety linked to making the wrong decision. The operational conditions of successful decision making seem fairly straightforward: get started and keep the momentum going. Unfortunately, there is no one-size-fits-all recipe. Decision making requires a certain amount of courage and faith. This means that you might have to jump on before the train passes. Weigh the pros and cons, make your decision, and do not look back. Living your life in the rearview mirror will not change the course of events. Instead, it will adversely affect you and your future ability to move on and seize new opportunities (before they are gone).

One of the few upsides of this bitter lesson for me was not to take rejection personally. The fact that the position was filled by someone else had nothing to do with my performance in the job meeting. Instead, it had everything to do with my behavior outside of it. My loss was someone else's gain. Another candidate down the list randomly received the job proposal that I was initially presented with. Momentum can sometimes be the decisive factor.

I have been through many job interviews. Those which ended unfavorably always triggered a wave of auto-criticism. In my mind, I replayed what I could have done differently if only the moment could be repeated. "If I could turn back time" is a great song, but Cher's words ring painfully true for all those who have ever allowed their moment to pass. Post-mortem analysis might work in retrospect. It helps to mitigate the risk of similar mistakes being made in the future. What it will not teach is how to seize the momentum. The next time you negotiate, perform a pre-mortem instead. A pre-mortem is a fictional scenario in which you anticipate that a project or undertaking has failed. Imagining what you could lose if the best preventive measure from it happening.

Guideline 25—Key Takeaways
1. Learn to spot opportunities before they are gone.
2. Allow yourself the time to part with the known, but do not get stuck in the transition between the old and the new reality for too long.
3. Get started and keep the momentum going.
4. Weigh the pros and cons, make a decision, and do not look back.
5. Perform a pre-mortem and seize the momentum.

GUIDELINE 26

The Power of Eight

JUST outside the city of Geneva, Switzerland, there is a small town called Prangins. On a hill above the village, overlooking the turquoise waters of Lake Geneva and offering breathtaking views of the French Chablais Alps, stands the Château de Prangins (the Prangins Castle, completed in its present form around 1730). It used to house Voltaire and Joseph Bonaparte. Since 1998, it is home to the Swiss National Museum, which has become a heritage site of national significance. Small jewels of insight can be found in the most unexpected places.

Room 5 of the museum is dedicated to Bourgeois Life. The word *bourgeois* can trigger negative connotations. Therefore, the term needs to be clearly defined in order to avoid any misinterpretations, both in terms of meaning and intent. It depicts people from a social class with specific cultural and financial capital, living in the urban area, who owned means of production, and valued property and preservation of capital as a way of ensuring their economic supremacy. My aim is not to judge nor favor any social class but rather to provide an example of the link between certain values and what they can lead to.

Going back to the exhibit hall, the room itself displays a salon from around 1850 with several portraits and pieces of furniture from the era. The real item of interest is the leaflet and the description it provides: "The bourgeois way of life, available only to a small minority of the population, followed a carefully balanced pattern of work and play, effort and relaxation. In all matters the outstanding bourgeois virtues were order, cleanliness, industry and punctuality."

The sequence of the visit is intriguing. The next exhibit hall is Room 6. Its description sheds some light on how Switzerland became one of the world's strongest economies. During the 19th century, the country changed its focus from a rural community to a city-based society. Banks, among other institutions, established their headquarters in rapidly growing towns. In terms of the global economy, no other country exported as many industrial products worldwide as Switzerland in relation to the modest size of its population.

Two things caught my attention when I was visiting the museum: the importance of balancing work and leisure, and secondly, the guidelines aka principles that can be applied to achieving goals. Bridging the work-life balance (that I prefer to see as a fit, not a balance—see Guideline 11), combined with a system of virtues, seemed to work out quite well for the Swiss. Could this be the recipe for entrepreneurial success?

This book is a recollection of my professional experiences. I taught myself by implementing first. I continue to learn my way through life by making mistakes and finding ways to do things better. Bad decisions coupled with good reflections can produce satisfactory future outcomes. Let us go back to the octopus drawing interview one last time since this is what we started with. As it turns out, eight is a special number. It is the symbol of infinity and harmony due to the balance of the two interlocking loops. Eight is also considered a symbol of self-confidence, success, inner wisdom, and financial abundance. It is associated with such traits as decisiveness, self-discipline, efficiency, and prosperity.

The symbolism of eight is universal. According to the Bible, this number is a symbol of creation and new beginnings. In Asian cultures, it is said to invite great wealth. The lucky stones are amethyst, black diamond, and pearls. Number eight means that you are on the right path to reaching your objectives. The interview fiasco certainly confirmed that for me.

According to the Merriam-Webster dictionary, a guideline is "a line by which one is guided: such as, (a) cord or rope to aid a passer over a difficult point or to permit retracing a course; (b) an indication or outline of policy or conduct." I am passing you the line in the hope that these guidelines can serve as a foundation for behavior that will get you what you want out of your professional life and beyond. May the octo-power guide you!

Guideline 26—Key Takeaways

1. Be open to inspiration in unexpected places.

2. Introduce discipline into your life.

3. Bridge your life goals with a system of principles.

4. Make mistakes and find ways to do things better.

5. Embrace eight as the symbol of self-confidence, success, inner wisdom, and financial abundance.

Interview Insights

Now that we have gone through the guidelines that will help boost your career, I would like to share a few more insights from my interview for the Marketing Insider Review.[5] The questions are a nutshell reflection of the most frequently addressed issues that surface in negotiations. These aspects defied categorization into a specific guideline category, yet they reflect some of the themes discussed throughout the book. I hope they will cover any areas that I might have missed and will allow you to systematize the learnings from a spectator perspective.

When did the interest in negotiation arise in you?
Prof. Dr. Jagodzinska: I hold a PhD in law. A major part of the legal profession is related to negotiations. I developed an interest in the topic of negotiation during my scholarship in Nice, in France. I think it was then that I realized that I want to gain more knowledge in the field of negotiations and combine theory and practice.

Are you treated differently in a negotiation because you are a woman?
Prof. Dr. Jagodzinska: I have been blessed to cross paths with mentors and business partners who value me for my achievements and professional conduct. When I lecture the future generation of managers, the values that I convey to them are based on gender equality and equal opportunities. Consequently, in my business activities, I avoid interactions with people who display any forms of gender discrimination.

Is the art of negotiation easier for any gender?
Prof. Dr. Jagodzinska: Each negotiator is different and cannot be classified based on gender alone. Nonetheless, stereotypes reflect a collective memory of certain predominant patterns of behavior of a

---

[5] https://www.marketinginsiderreview.com/kasia-jagodzinska-consultora-internacional/

specific group. Therefore, it is helpful to know what they are in order to rise above the limitations they carry. Furthermore, recognition of gender differences may allow negotiators of both sexes to maximize their diversity in reaching better agreements.

When did we start negotiating in our lives?

Prof. Dr. Jagodzinska: The most basic aim of a negotiation is to have certain needs met. In that sense, we all started out as master negotiators the moment we were born. It was sufficient to demand attention to have the basic needs satisfied. Obviously, as we mature, we have to find more refined ways of negotiating and obtaining the desired outcomes.

Do we need to know how the brain works to negotiate well?

Prof. Dr. Jagodzinska: The brain is built in such a way that when an external trigger enters, it first reaches the amygdala, which is a cluster of neurons located in the brain's medial temporal lobe that forms part of the limbic system. The amygdala plays a key role in processing emotions. In a very simplified illustration, once the trigger passes the amygdala, it reaches the neocortex, which is a region responsible for, among others, cognition, perception, and logical reasoning. Contrary to what we would like to think, biology suggests that humans are primarily emotional beings.

What are the most important rules that a good negotiator must follow?

Prof. Dr. Jagodzinska: Respect for their negotiation partner, an open mind, flexible approach, and solid preparation.

What other factors are important in a business negotiation?

Prof. Dr. Jagodzinska: A negotiation consists of the task and the relationship-oriented aspects. For long-lasting agreements, there needs to be a balance between the task and the relationship between the parties. Focus on achieving the desired negotiation outcome (task) will not be sufficient for securing a durable business arrangement. Conversely, making concessions for the sake of preserving the relationship will only lead to disenchantment in the long term. A skilled negotiator needs to understand how to bridge both aspects.

A tip for those who want to negotiate with other professionals?

Prof. Dr. Jagodzinska: To successfully conclude a business conversation, negotiation skills, and tactics are often not enough. If you enter a negotiation with fear, self-doubt, or lack of conviction, you will not win no matter how well tactically you have been trained. You need to equip yourself with the self-management toolkit that will allow you to tame emotions, ego, and stress in a negotiation. My methodology, Negotiation Booster (www.negotiationbooster.com), was developed to help negotiators thrive in their negotiations by means of personal empowerment.

Summary of Guidelines

Guideline 1: My career track looks like an octopus

Key Takeaways
1. Do not be misled by impression management.
2. Beware of the priming effect and consciously control it.
3. Understand the real drivers of your behavior.
4. Prepare for the unexpected.
5. Think first, then act.
6. Learn how to draw.

Guideline 2: Do not settle for less than what feels right

Key Takeaways
1. Pay attention to your instincts.
2. Be creative when you explore your career options.
3. Do not be afraid to go off the beaten track.
4. Seek advice from a third party.
5. Control your ego.
6. If you have to settle, settle for more rather than less.

Guideline 3: Set the bar high

Key Takeaways
1. Create demand for your offering.
2. Pay attention to the context of the negotiation.
3. Know the reason behind the sacrifices you make.
4. "Over"-qualify yourself.
5. Craft many alternative options.
6. Never compromise on your expectations.

Guideline 4: Motivate yourself to exceed expectations

Key Takeaways
1. Make motivation a perpetual process.
2. Find out what motivates you most (competition, comparison, reward).
3. Allow loss aversion to fuel you to action.
4. Let second-level outcomes guide you toward your goal.
5. Exceed expectations.

Guideline 5: Success loves company

Key Takeaways
1. Secure one success and the next one will follow.
2. Attract what you want by letting go.
3. Do not be afraid of change; this is when it all starts.
4. Be open to creative arrangements; they will open new doors for you.
5. Accept that (temporarily) life-work balance may be a myth.

Guideline 6: Get the best job title

Key Takeaways
1. Avoid cryptic titles.
2. Never accept a lower title in exchange for a higher salary.
3. Choose a clear, universal, and easily understood title.
4. Negotiate the best possible title.
5. Let the title be a source of your inner power.

Guideline 7: Never stop looking for new career opportunities

Key Takeaways
1. Make career searching a life-long habit.
2. Develop strategies for personal empowerment.
3. Equip yourself with information about the job market.
4. Make an inventory of your knowledge, skills, and abilities.
5. Craft multiple creative options for your career.

Guideline 8: Develop your natural talents

Key Takeaways
1. Focus on your strengths, not weaknesses.
2. Distribute your energy in the most efficient manner.
3. Find out what you do not like and make a change.
4. Discover what you enjoy doing (and what you are good at).
5. Maximize your natural talents.

Guideline 9: Build your army of supporters

Key Takeaways
1. Invest time and have the patience to build trust.
2. Remember that business is personal.
3. "Assume positive intent."
4. Apply the law of reciprocity.
5. Give more than you take.
6. Rely on your network for support.

Guideline 10: Get a tough mentor

Key Takeaways
1. A mentor is like a commander—they are your security blanket.
2. They need to be emotionally stable to be able to stabilize you.
3. Choose someone you will trust and see as an authority figure.
4. Rely on their judgment—things look different from an objective view.
5. Tough love will make you stronger.

Guideline 11: Never compromise on your values

Key Takeaways
1. Compromise is a win-lose strategy.
2. No gain is worth the loss of your personal values.
3. Build and protect your integrity.
4. Find a work-life fit.
5. Cut off situations that are detrimental to your system of values.

Guideline 12: Design your personal brand of excellence

Key Takeaways
1. Use your unique skillset to build your own personal brand.
2. Do not allow yourself (or others) to downplay your status or downgrade your power.
3. Enter a negotiation with command presence.
4. Work in the service of your personal brand.
5. Let your personal brand play first chair.

Guideline 13: Expand your horizons

Key Takeaways
1. Keep developing even if you are not yet clear about what you want to do.
2. Once you set a goal, channel all your efforts to achieve it.
3. Invest time in the most efficient manner.
4. Be ready to pay the price for going off the beaten track.
5. Build up your unique talent stack.

Guideline 14: Learn to live one day at a time

Key Takeaways
1. Do not attempt to plan where you will be in x number of years.
2. Learn to let go by adopting a flexible approach to life.
3. Live in the moment but do not get locked in it.
4. Do not take anything for granted.
5. Develop patterns of behavior that will bring you closer to your overall goals.

Guideline 15: Define your life non-negotiables

Key Takeaways
1. Make a list of your life demands.
2. Place the demands in order of importance.
3. Never negotiate down with yourself.
4. Respect your non-negotiables if you want others to acknowledge them.
5. Create value by setting your priorities.

Guideline 16: Project the outcome you want

Key Takeaways
1. Use visualization to achieve the goals you set in your life negotiations.
2. Project the future you want by displaying it on a vision board.
3. Use this formula: "By [input date], I will achieve [insert what you want]."
4. Create anticipatory emotions by pasting your pictures next to your dreams.
5. Take necessary action to tick off the elements on your board.

Guideline 17: Develop high-performance habits

Key Takeaways
1. Develop healthy habits as early as possible.
2. Instill good habits by proper scene-setting.
3. Exercise the freedom to choose the (good) habit that you want to develop.
4. Ingrain a (good) habit by introducing the element of enjoyment.
5. Cultivate activities that develop emotional stability, require a proactive approach and multi dimensional outlook, and stimulate positive energy.

Guideline 18: Frequent the best places

Key Takeaways
1. Reward yourself for your efforts.
2. Get a taste of the good life.
3. Go to the best places to soak up the atmosphere.
4. Expose yourself to positive stimuli (people, events, places, nature).
5. Prime yourself for success.

Guideline 19: Build an aura of desirability

Key Takeaways
1. Invest in superior quality.
2. Make high standards become the norm for yourself.
3. Prime your negotiation partner before making an offer.
4. Pay attention to details.
5. Create your own and unique brand, then make it an object of desire.

Guideline 20: Dress for success

Key Takeaways
1. Focus on self-impression before you attempt to manage external impressions.
2. Dress the part to become the part.
3. Do not wait until you are successful to start looking like it.
4. Let dress be your armor—it serves as camouflage for your mental insecurities and inner doubts.
5. Design a strong, concise, and professional profile (a few lines at the beginning of your CV and as a title on your professional social media).

Guideline 21: Life is a journey (aka the airplane test)

Key Takeaways
1. Increase your likeability factor.
2. Have your elevator pitch ready—who you are, what you do, and what you are looking to do.
3. Travel light—free of negative emotional baggage.
4. Be open to networking opportunities wherever life takes you.
5. Upgrade to personal business class.

Guideline 22: Communicate like a boss

Key Takeaways
1. Beware of the misrepresentation effect.
2. Develop the ability to listen effectively.
3. Listen beyond the words.
4. Look for signs of the ego and feed it.
5. Communicate like a boss without being bossy.

Guideline 23: Be selective

Key Takeaways
1. Develop your personality in parallel to growing your skillset.
2. Be choosy about who you associate with on a personal and professional level.
3. Perform a personal return on investment (PROI) analysis before you accept a job offer.
4. Structure your job search in an efficient manner.
5. Make sure that the job fulfills your objectives and serves as a springboard for success and further growth.

Guideline 24: Build trust

Key Takeaways
1. Establish a thread of trust at the beginning of the relationship.
2. Work together with the other party to establish trust and strengthen it by reliable interactions.
3. Build the characteristics of a trustworthy individual: professional and personal competence, reliability, integrity, honesty and openness, a caring and respectful attitude, and integrity.
4. Take care not to ruin the trust.
5. Separate the task from the relationship.

Guideline 25: Momentum is everything

Key Takeaways
1. Learn to spot opportunities before they are gone.
2. Allow yourself the time to part with the known, but do not get stuck in the transition between the old and the new reality for too long.
3. Get started and keep the momentum going.
4. Weigh the pros and cons, make a decision, and do not look back.
5. Perform a pre-mortem and seize the momentum.

Guideline 26: The power of eight

Key Takeaways
1. Be open to inspiration in unexpected places.
2. Introduce discipline into your life.
3. Bridge your life goals with a system of principles.
4. Make mistakes and find ways to do things better.
5. Embrace eight as the symbol of self-confidence, success, inner wisdom, and financial abundance.

References for Further Reading

Adams, S. 2017. *Win Bigly. Persuasion in a World Where Facts Don't Matter*. New York: Portfolio/Penguin.

Annis, B., and J. Gray. 2013. *Work With Me. How Gender Intelligence Can Help You Succeed at Work and in Life*. London: Piatkus.

Barker, A. 2016. *Improve Your Communication Skills*. New York: Kogan Page Limited.

Carnegie, D. 2006. *How to Win Friends and Influence People*. London: Vermilion.

Cialdini, R. 2016. *Pre-Suasion. A Revolutionary Way to Influence and Persuade*. London: Random House Books.

Collins, P. 2009. *Talking Your Way to What You Want. Negotiate to Win!* New York, NY: Sterling Publishing.

Dalio, R. 2017. *Principles: Life and Work*. New York, NY: Simon & Schuster.

Dawson, R. 2011. *Secrets of Power Negotiating. Updated for the 21st Century*. New Jersey, NJ: The Career Press.

Dinnar, S., and L. Susskind. 2019. *Entrepreneurial Negotiation: Understanding and Managing the Relationships that Determine Your Entrepreneurial Success*. New York, NY: Springer.

Duhigg, C. 2014. *The Power of Habit. Why We Do What We Do in Life and in Business*. New York, NY: Random House Trade Paperbacks.

Fisher, R., and D. Shapiro. 2005. *Beyond Reason. Using Emotions as You Negotiate*. London: Penguin Books.

Fleming, K. 2016. *The Leader's Guide to Emotional Agility. How to Use Soft Skills to Get Hard Results*. Harlow: Pearson Education Limited.

Gino, F. 2019. *Rebel Talent. Why it Pays to Break the Rules at Work and in Life*. London: Pan Books.

Hicks, D. 2019. *Leading with Dignity: How to Create a Culture that Brings Out the Best in People*. Yale University Press.

Hill, N. 2005. *Think and Grow Rich*. New York, NY: Jeremy P. Tarcher/Penguin.

Holiday, R. 2016. *Ego is the Enemy. The Fight to Master Our Greatest Opponent*. London: Profile Books Ltd.

Jagodzinska, K. 2021. *Negotiation Booster. The Ultimate Self-Empowerment Guide to High-Impact Negotiations*. New York: Business Expert Press.

Jagodzinska, K. 2016. "Egotiation is the New Negotiation: The Concept of Negotiation Revisited". *Eurasian Journal of Business and Management* 4, no. 2, 72–80. doi: 10.15604/ejss.2016.04.02.007

Jagodzinska, K. 2016. "How to Manage Perception to Win Negotiations". *International Journal of Social Science Studies* 4, no. 2, 69–77. doi: 10.11114/ijsss.v4i2.1320

Jang, J. 2015. *Rejection Proof. How to Beat Fear and Become Invincible.* London: Random House.

Mayer, B. 2000. *The Dynamics of Conflict Resolution.* A Practitioner's Guide. Jossey-Bass.

Morgan, N. 2013. "How to Become an Authentic Speaker". *HBR's 10 Must Reads on Communication.* Boston, Massachusetts: Harvard Business Review Press.

Also by Kasia Jagodzinska:

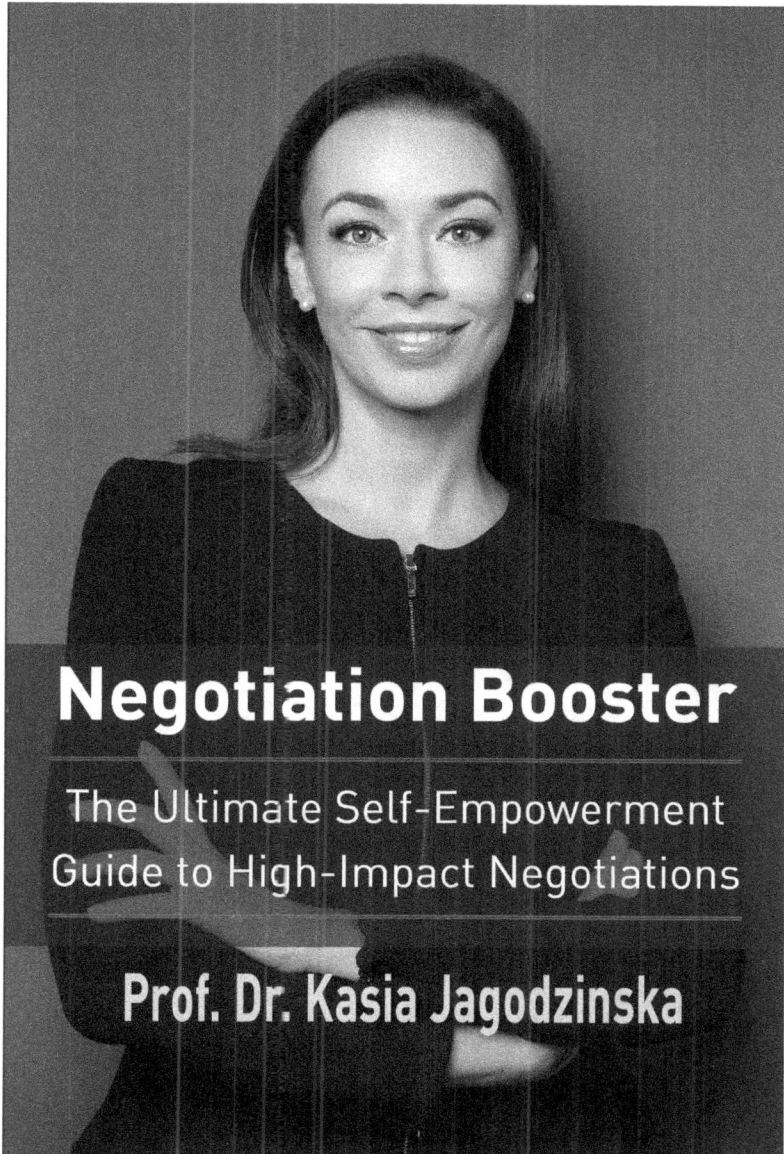

Negotiation Booster

The Ultimate Self-Empowerment
Guide to High-Impact Negotiations

Prof. Dr. Kasia Jagodzinska

Negotiation Booster: The Ultimate Self-Empowerment Guide to High-Impact Negotiations

Book Abstract

To successfully conclude a business conversation, negotiation skills and tactics are often not enough. If you enter a negotiation with fear, self-doubt or lack of conviction, you will not win no matter how well tactically you have been trained. Negotiation Booster is a novel approach that leverages the task related aspects of a negotiation with the underlying emotional factors. It is the ultimate guide to winning negotiations by means of self-empowerment.

The distinguishing features of Negotiation Booster are as follows:

I.   It introduces an interdisciplinary approach to the topic of negotiation: the book explores fundamental negotiation tactics, communication, perception and impression management techniques, the determinants of desired outcomes and the issues that negotiators face internally and externally in the negotiation process;

II.   It equips the reader with practical tips on how to navigate around real-life challenges and avoid the most common mistakes that negotiators make;

III.   It is a compilation of the experiences shared by business professionals of the biggest companies from Europe, Asia, the Middle East, and the United States;

IV.   It breaks down the negotiation process into four phases: Primer, Shadowing, Sealer, Implementor and delivers tips on how to succeed in each of them;

V.   It provides a straightforward and user-friendly framework for strategic preparation and monitoring of progress (The Negotiation Matrix).

Index

OTHER TITLES IN THE BUSINESS CAREER DEVELOPMENT COLLECTION

Vilma Barr, Consultant, Editor

- *How to Make Good Business Decisions* by J.C. Baker
- *The Power of Belonging* by Sunita Sehmi
- *Emotional Intelligence at Work* by Richard M. Contino, and Penelope J. Holt
- *Your GPS to Employment Success* by Beverly A. Williams
- *The Champion Edge* by Alan R. Zimmerman
- *Shaping Your Future* by Rita Rocker-Craft
- *Finding Your Career Niche* by Anne S. Klein
- *The Trust Factor* by Russell von Frank
- *Creating A Business and Personal Legacy* by Mark J. Munoz
- *Innovative Selling* by Eden White
- *Present! Connect!* by Tom Guggino
- *Introduction to Business* by Patrice Flynn
- *Be Different!* by Stan Silverman
- *Strategic Bootstrapping* by Matthew W. Rutherford

Announcing the Business Expert Press Digital Library

Concise e-books business students need for classroom and research

This book can also be purchased in an e-book collection by your library as

- a one-time purchase,
- that is owned forever,
- allows for simultaneous readers,
- has no restrictions on printing, and
- can be downloaded as PDFs from within the library community.

Our digital library collections are a great solution to beat the rising cost of textbooks. E-books can be loaded into their course management systems or onto students' e-book readers.
The **Business Expert Press** digital libraries are very affordable, with no obligation to buy in future years. For more information, please visit **www.businessexpertpress.com/librarians**. To set up a trial in the United States, please email **sales@businessexpertpress.com**.

www.ingramcontent.com/pod-product-compliance
Lightning Source LLC
Chambersburg PA
CBHW061335220326
41599CB00026B/5194